Three Literary Friendships

Also by John Lehmann

Collected Poems
Virginia Woolf and Her World
Edward Lear and His World
A Nest of Tigers
The Strange Destiny of Rupert Brooke
The Whispering Gallery
I Am My Brother
The Ample Proposition
In My Own Time
Thrown to the Woolfs
English Poets of the First World War
New Writing (Ed.)

John Lehmann

Three Literary Friendships

Byron & Shelley
Rimbaud & Verlaine
Robert Frost & Edward Thomas

A William Abrahams Book
Holt, Rinehart and Winston
New York

Copyright © 1983 by John Lehmann
All rights reserved, including the right to
reproduce this book or portions thereof in any form.
First published in the United States in 1984 by
Holt, Rinehart and Winston,
383 Madison Avenue,
New York, New York 10017.

Library of Congress Cataloging in Publication Data
Lehmann, John, 1907–
Three literary friendships.
"A William Abrahams book."
Bibliography: p.
Includes index.
1. Poets—Relations with men.   2. Friendship.
I. Title.   II. Title: Literary friendships.
PN452.L43   1984   809.1'9353   83-22658
ISBN 0-03-061593-3

First American Edition
Printed in the United States of America
1 3 5 7 9 10 8 6 4 2

The author wishes to make grateful
acknowledgement for use of portions of
the following:
"The Death of the Hired Man" from *The Poetry
of Robert Frost* edited by Edward Connery
Lathem. Copyright 1930, 1939, © 1969 by Holt,
Rinehart and Winston. Copyright © 1958 by
Robert Frost. Copyright © 1967 by Lesley Frost
Ballantine. Reprinted by permission of Holt,
Rinehart and Winston, Publishers.
Selected Letters of Robert Frost edited by
Lawrance Thompson. Copyright © 1964 by
Lawrance Thompson and Holt, Rinehart and
Winston. Reprinted by permission of Holt,
Rinehart and Winston, Publishers.
The letters of Edward Thomas reprinted by
permission of Myfanwy Thomas.

ISBN 0-03-061593-3

Contents

Three Literary Friendships

Introduction

One of the most intriguing aspects of modern poetry – and by that I mean the poetry of the last 200 years – is the way in which two outstanding and highly gifted poets have come together for one reason or another – living proximity (often by chance), or the discovery of close spiritual affinity – and for a certain number of years have influenced one another in their being and art, and indeed brought out the best, perhaps the unexpected best, in one another's gifts. I make at once the confession that this process has always deeply fascinated me, and at the same time the admission that such mutual influence is not easy to detect or define, and one has to be guided as much by intuition and imagination as by recorded fact.

That such mutual influence and stimulation existed in earlier periods cannot of course be denied, nor can it be proved. It seems evident in what we know of the Elizabethan and Jacobean drama; but the details we would like to have are altogether lost. To what extent Shakespeare, for instance, collaborated with other dramatists in certain plays, our suspicions often only aroused by a few lines here or there, must always remain a matter at the best of intelligent surmise. Much as one would like to explore this field, it remains on the whole an unprofitable enterprise, until such time – if ever – as more documents come to light. How wonderful to discover a working notebook of Shakespeare's!

In this book I have concentrated on three examples which are to my mind of the first importance in European poetry since the Romantic Revival. First, the coming together of Byron and Shelley in Switzerland and Italy at a time when both poets were approaching the height of their powers; second, the circumstances which brought together two French poets, Paul Verlaine and Arthur Rimbaud, in the seventies of the last century, in circumstances that were as scandalous to the *bien pensants* of the day as they were productive in poetry, and which were to have an influence on subsequent European poetry, the ripples of which have still not ceased to spread, not least in English poetry; the third, the happy accident which led to the friendship between an American poet, Robert Frost, who was already thirty-eight and still without renown or recognition in his own country, and an English writer who had written only prose until then, but who soon after this friendship began, in 1913–14, started to write the poems that have made the name of Edward Thomas one of the most illustrious and most profoundly admired in the poetry of that epoch. My own feeling is that the significance of his work has not yet been fully appreciated.

I

Donny Johnny
&
The Serpent

Byron & Shelley

If one had been alive during the years immediately following the battle of Waterloo, nothing would have seemed more extraordinary than the friendship that grew up between Lord Byron and Percy Bysshe Shelley; nor that it was engineered in its origin by a rather silly young woman, Claire Clairmont, who had made up her mind to be Byron's mistress.

They were both poets, but one was already famous: *Childe Harold*, a poem that had rocked London – and eventually the world – on the publication in 1812 of its first cantos, had made Byron famous overnight; while Shelley's first long poem, *Queen Mab*, published in 1813, had been reviled by all the critics and made no reputation at all, save disgrace, for its twenty-one-year-old author. Byron, four years older, was a member of a fashionable fast London set, who turned their backs on him when scandal began to circulate about his relations with his half-sister Augusta Leigh, and his ill-treatment of the wife he had only recently married. Shelley was known only to a small bohemian circle of poetasters and critics, and did not hesitate to proclaim himself a radical in politics and an atheist, at a time when reaction, after the Napoleonic Wars, was supreme.

And yet there were factors that united them. Both had been to public schools, Shelley to Eton and Byron to Harrow, and both had therefore a training in the Classics. Byron was well versed in the Latin authors, but Shelley, who had the finer intellect, knew the Greeks and their philosophy and poetry far more deeply than Byron. Equally important was the fact that they both came out of the top drawer: Byron as a peer of the realm, and Shelley as the heir to a baronetcy. Both had money of their own: Byron from family inheritances, in addition to what he earned by his poetry – sums which steadily increased as his fame increased; and Shelley from the allowance made by his father and from what he borrowed on his expectations – which were large. Both were generous to relatives and dependants, and to others who had only the most tenuous claim on their generosity. Byron liked to live like a lord, splashing his money about on domestic extravagances, mistresses and a retinue of servants (and a menagerie which accompanied him wherever he went and appeared to have a free run of the house wherever he might settle). Shelley preferred to live simply, with Mary Wollstonecraft Godwin, whom he married following the death (probably by suicide) of his first wife, Harriet Westbrook, after he had quite callously abandoned her when he fell in love with Mary. The third person in the Shelley household was Claire Clairmont, Mary's stepsister. Both poets had fallen foul of the moral establishment of the time. Claire had already forced herself on Byron in England, and was pregnant with his child. She had every reason to want to track down the father, and the decision of Shelley and Mary to make an expedition on the continent rather than to Scotland, which had been their first idea, gave her the opportunity. She knew that Byron intended to stay on the Lake of Geneva, and she persuaded Shelley, a devoted admirer of Rousseau, to stop off there. Her whole scheme depended on bringing the two poets together. Luck favoured her.

Byron had left England – as it happened for ever – towards the end of April. Shelley and his party reached Geneva on 13 May 1816, and put up at the Hôtel d'Angleterre (now demolished*), which had a high reputation as the best of the local hotels with fine gardens that led down to the lakeside, and a view of Mont Blanc. Boats could be hired there, for rowing or sailing about the lake, an amenity that Shelley, with his passion for the water, was not slow to take advantage of.

Twelve days later Byron arrived with his retinue, which now included a young personal physician, Dr John Polidori, who was vain and hysterical and whose tantrums irritated Byron so much that he eventually sent him home. Claire, who had scanned the hotel register every day with the greatest care, now laid her plans. Very soon after he arrived, Byron began to row about the lake to look for a house to rent, and generally returned late in the afternoon, which was the time when Shelley and Mary and Claire liked to walk about the gardens. It was therefore not difficult for her to arrange that Shelley should be near the boathouse when Byron came back. Introductions followed, and it seems that the two poets took to one another at once. That first evening of their acquaintance they dined together, and it was not long before they formed the habit of taking breakfast together.

*All that remains is a small ancillary building and a plaque on the front gates, which records that Byron, Shelley and Ruskin stayed there, also an assortment of Royal personages including Queen Victoria.

Byron had been particularly attracted by a house near
Coligny, almost opposite on the other side of the lake,
which belonged to the Diodati family. After some hesitation
and rather tiresome negotiations, Byron signed a six-month
lease for the handsome villa with its large stable buildings
behind, which still stands on an eminence above the lake
though now lacking the elegant veranda on the first floor.
Shelley was also looking for a house, and eventually decided
on one at Montalègre, only a few minutes' walk from the
Villa Diodati lower down near the shore. Under this
arrangement they could continue to meet every day and
converse on every subject under the sun, without being
watched or overheard by the gossip-greedy tourists; though
the proprietor of the Hôtel d'Angleterre is said to have
provided, for a small charge, spy-glasses through which the
villa could be scanned and the appearance of the noble lord
and his guests on the balcony avidly observed. Thus a great
friendship, of complementary rather than of like minds,
began, perhaps the most important and fruitful in their two
short lives.

The two poets sailed about the lake together in a boat that
Shelley had hired. They enjoyed one another's company so
much that it was not long before they decided to make a
longer expedition round the lake, taking with them only two
boatmen and a servant, and with the aim of visiting all the
places that had been hallowed for them by Rousseau's *La
Nouvelle Héloïse*, and also the famous Castle of Chillon,
which inspired Byron to write one of his most brilliant and
moving shorter poems. For this longer expedition they
bought a small two-masted yacht. They left their
womenfolk behind. Though Byron had taken a liking to
Mary, whom he found as sensible as she was intelligent, he

was glad to escape from the importunities of Claire, who all too evidently regarded herself as his *maîtresse en titre*. Later, Byron in a letter to his sister Augusta, played the relationship down:

> As to all these mistresses, Lord help me, I have had but one. Now don't scold, but what could I do? – a foolish girl, in spite of all I could say or do, would come after me, or rather went before – for I found her here . . . I was not in love, nor have any love left for any, but I could not exactly play the Stoic with a woman who had scrambled eight hundred miles to unphilosophise me.

The weather on the lake was uncertain and subject to sudden squalls and violent choppiness. Shelley, oddly enough, could not swim, but does not seem to have been caused any anxiety by this disability. On one occasion, when their boat was in some danger as it approached a landing place, Byron told Shelley that if he didn't struggle he could easily save him. 'We were then about a hundred yards from shore and the boat in peril,' he wrote to Murray. 'He answered me with the greatest coolness, that he had no notion of being saved, and that I would have enough to do to save myself, and begged not to trouble me.'

Ever since he had left England, Byron was fitfully at work on the third canto of *Childe Harold*, which contains the famous passage on the eve of Waterloo. The canto was in a certain sense a travel diary, and announces Harold's arrival on the lake – 'Lake Leman woos me with its crystal face' – in its sixty-eighth stanza. Later, Byron told Medwin that Shelley did his best during their discussions to convert him to an admiration for Wordsworth, and 'used to dose me with Wordsworth physic even to nausea' as he jokingly put it; and one cannot read the remainder of the canto without a sense of the Wordsworthian attitude to nature echoing under some of the descriptions and turns of phrase, as in the seventy-second stanza:

> I live not in myself, but I become
> Portion of that around me; and to me
> High mountains are a feeling, but the hum
> Of human cities torture: I can see
> Nothing to loathe in nature, save to be
> A link reluctant in a fleshly chain,
> Classed among creatures, where the soul can flee,
> And with the sky, the peak, the heaving plain
> Of ocean, or the stars, mingle and not in vain . . .

Or this exceptionally beautiful passage, between stanzas eighty-six and eighty-seven, which was also recorded by Mary Shelley:

> There breathes a living fragrance from the shore,
> Of flowers yet fresh with childhood; on the ear
> Drops the light drip of the suspended oar,
> Or chirps the grasshopper one good-night carol more;
>
> He is an evening reveller, who makes
> His life an infancy, and sings his fill;
> At intervals, some bird from out the brakes
> Starts into voice a moment, then is still.

On 21 July Shelley and Mary went off for a week's tour into the mountains, and when they were at Chamonix

Shelley wrote his poem 'Mont Blanc', which with the 'Hymn to Intellectual Beauty' marks the beginning of his poetic maturity. At about this time Byron began to pay visits to Madame de Staël's salon at the Château de Coppet, a few miles from Geneva on the road to Nyon (and still in the same family), and old friends from London began to appear on the lake; John Cam Hobhouse and Scrope Davies came towards the end of August. Byron must have felt that these reminders of his former carefree and extravagant life in London would not have mixed very easily with the intellectual tone of his new friends, Shelley and Mary. He does not appear to have attempted to bring them together: nor does he seem to have taken Shelley with him to join Madame de Staël's gatherings. In any case the Shelleys had decided to return to England, and left on 29 August bearing with them the third canto of *Childe Harold*. The trust that had grown up between the two poets is shown by nothing more clearly than the *carte blanche* Byron gave Shelley in the negotiations with John Murray, as well as the permission he gave him to make small alterations in the text wherever he thought it advisable, and to see the proofs through the press. As far as the price for the poems went – and they were to include 'The Prisoner of Chillon' – Shelley acted in concert with Byron's reliable business friend, Douglas Kinnaird. They succeeded in persuading Murray to give £2,000 instead of the £1,200 originally proposed; a bargain that appeared to rankle with Murray, for a year later, astonishingly, he described Shelley as 'the vilest wretch now living'. In any case he cannot have lost by the bargain: the third canto of *Childe Harold* was published on 18 November, and 'The Prisoner of Chillon' on 5 December. About 7,000 copies of each were sold on the day of publication. The 'ineffectual angel' had proved himself quite a match for the canny Scottish publisher.

During the three months they had been together in Switzerland Shelley had acquired a deep respect for Byron's genius as a poet. He had already come to the conclusion that, fine as *Childe Harold* was, Byron was capable of something much finer; something that would show to the world his many-sided gifts more effectively, his humour, his keen observation of the world side by side with his romantic sensibility, and his extraordinary facility in the craft of verse-making. What he wanted above all was that Byron should show himself to be a serious poet, rather than a brilliantly talented performer acting out the 'Byronic' role that had brought him his early fame. 'I hope for no more than that you should,' he wrote to Byron, 'find that you are chosen out from all other men to some greater enterprise of thought; and that all your studies should, from that moment, tend towards that enterprise alone: that your affections, that all worldly hopes this world may have left you, should link themselves to this design.' Such empathetic encouragement must have been frequently repeated in their talks and boating excursions on the lake. Byron had a shallower side, as Shelley detected, and he set himself to rouse Byron's ambition beyond that level. That Shelley spoke with absolutely selfless conviction is beyond doubt: his enthusiasm for *Don Juan* when at last that great poem was entered upon, a poem that was totally different from and beyond Shelley's range, is proof of his disinterestedness – and perspicacity.

It was nearly two years before they came together again, though Byron must have written to Shelley, particularly about Claire, but his letters have disappeared. In a letter to

Kinnaird – from Diodati – at the end of September, he wrote: 'Pray continue to like Shelley – he is a very good – very clever – but a very singular man – he was a great comfort to me here by his intelligence and good nature.' This continued to be Byron's attitude towards Shelley to the very end, though their relations were complicated and made extremely delicate owing to the rôle Shelley took upon himself of acting as Claire's intermediary after the birth of Allegra in January 1817.

Byron moved on to Venice and made the Palazzo Mocenigo his home, while Shelley decided to settle in Marlow, on the Thames, to be near Peacock, who admired him and gave him sound advice on his practical affairs. At this stage in his life the presence of someone like Peacock was extremely valuable to him; a stage that included the tragic death of Harriet, and the long and painful legal negotiations which ended in the custodianship of his children by Harriet being taken away from him, and his marriage to Mary. During his visits to London Shelley became a very close friend to Leigh Hunt, and at Hunt's house met many of the leading lights of literary London, including Keats. Shelley was at once aware of Keats's great potentialities as a poet, but Keats was wary of Shelley and hypersensitive, one cannot help thinking, about class-differences between them.

One other fellow guest at Hunt's house, who was to become one of Shelley's most sympathetic friends, was Horace Smith, author – with his brother James – of the brilliant series of parodies published in 1812 as *Rejected Addresses*. Horace Smith was by profession a stockbroker, but was deeply interested in the arts and wrote poetry and pastoral dramas himself. 'Is it not odd,' Shelley once observed to Hunt, 'that the only truly generous person I ever knew, who had money to be generous with, should be a stockbroker!' Horace Smith has left us some vivid impressions of Shelley at this time. Of his physical appearance he wrote that he was 'fair, freckled, blue-eyed, light-haired, delicate-looking', and, studying him carefully, continued:

His stature would have been rather tall had he carried himself upright; his earnest voice, though never loud, was somewhat unmusical. Manifest as it was that his pre-occupied mind had no thought to spare for the modish adjustment of his fashionably-made clothes, it was impossible to doubt, even for a moment, that you were gazing upon a *gentleman*; a first impression which subsequent observation never failed to confirm, even in the most exalted acceptation of the term, as indicating one that is gentle, generous, accomplished, brave . . .

Horace Smith appears in a glowing light in the poem Shelley addressed to Maria Gisborne in 1820, when he was occupying the Gisbornes' house in Livorno, describing the friends he hoped she would meet when she reached London: especially Leigh Hunt, Peacock, Hogg, and one in whom:

Wit and sense,
Virtue and human knowledge; all that might
Make this dull world a business of delight,
Are all combined in Horace Smith . . .

While they were at Marlow, staying with Peacock until the refurbishing of Albion House nearby should be completed, Shelley spent much of his time in his boat on the river, or in Bisham woods which rise on one side above it, writing his long poem *Laon and Cythna*, which appeared eventually, with the incest theme toned down, as *The Revolt of Islam*. But his mind was constantly occupied with the birth of Allegra, Claire's child by Byron, in Bath in January 1817, and the problems involved in getting Byron interested in his child and making some arrangement to look after her. As the result of complicated negotiations it was finally decided that the infant, accompanied by Shelley's Swiss nurse and under Shelley's own guardian eye, should be taken to Italy for Byron to decide her future with her presence before him. A further sound reason for this trip was the deterioration of Shelley's health: the doctors warned him that unless he had a change of climate he was in danger of serious consumption. On 11 March 1818 the company set forth for Italy: Shelley, Mary and her two young children, Claire, Allegra and their servants. The evening before they left they went to the opera, of which Shelley was especially fond, and a supper party followed with the Hunts and Peacock.

Shelley and his party did not reach Lyons until 21 March. They crossed the Mont Cenis into Italy on the 30th, and Shelley began his long and famous series of letters to Peacock describing their first impressions of Italy. In one of the earliest, written from Milan, he rhapsodizes about the almost miraculous effect the air and climate of Italy had upon his spirits and his health: 'No sooner had we arrived in Italy, than the loveliness of the earth and the serenity of the sky made the greatest difference in my sensations. I depend on these things for life; for in the smoke of cities, and the tumult of human kind, and the chilling fogs and rain of our own country, I can hardly be said to live.' They dawdled happily in Milan, and planned at first to settle on Lake Como, in the Villa Pliniana with its romantic setting and history. Shelley's idea appears to have been to lure Byron to visit them there and take his child back with him to Venice. But Byron was not so easily to be persuaded. He wanted to see his child, but he was not going to be involved with Claire again. A difficult exchange of letters took place. Finally Claire gave in, and it was arranged that Elise would take Allegra to Byron without Claire, after which the child should be entirely Byron's responsibility. If Shelley had known at that time of Byron's dissolute life in Venice, he might have proposed some other solution; as it was he realized Byron's implacable opposition to any arrangement which involved Claire's presence or proximity, and had no further arguments to put forward. On 28 April Elise started her journey to Venice with Allegra, and Shelley and Mary launched out on their further travels into Italy. They went to Pisa, and from there to Livorno which they found dreary enough. They moved to Bagni di Lucca for a few weeks, but Allegra was constantly in Shelley's mind, and to find out what Byron's plans were – without revealing to Byron that Claire was with them – he decided to call on him on 23 August.

Byron appears to have been delighted to see him, and, starved as he had been during the two years' interval of the kind of intellectual discussions he had so much enjoyed with Shelley in Geneva, insisted on his guest staying several nights, and offered him and Mary the villa at Este of which he had taken a lease, for as long as they liked. Byron persuaded Shelley to accompany him on his afternoon rides on the Lido, of which Shelley has left us a memorial in one of his most human and most vivid poems, 'Julian and Maddolo', one of the first fruits of the stimulus intimacy with Byron always gave him – a stimulus which also produced a far more characteristic poem in 'Lines Written among the Euganean Hills'.

'Julian and Maddolo' begins with a preface in which Maddolo is described as a Venetian nobleman 'of the most consummate genius', in whom 'his passions and his powers are incomparably greater than those of other men; and instead of the latter having been employed in curbing the former, they have mutually lent each other strength'. He describes him as 'cheerful, frank and witty', and his conversation as 'a sort of intoxication; men are held by it as a spell'. Julian, evidently to be taken as a portrait of himself, Shelley describes as an Englishman of good family, 'passionately attached to those philosophical notions which assert the power of man over his own mind . . . Without concealing the evil in the world, he is forever speculating how good may be made superior.' He sums him up as 'a complete infidel, and a scoffer at all things reported holy . . . What Maddolo thinks on these matters is not exactly known.'

In this preface Shelley is being remarkably fair to both Byron and himself, and the poem that follows gives the authentic impression of two men of exceptional mental powers and happiness in one another's company, arguing against one another yet without loss of harmony or humour. They embark in their gondola again after their ride, but the poem then turns to the incomparable beauty of the sunset over Venice and the Euganean Hills, and the conversation – of which one would have liked to hear so much more – begins to occupy itself with the madhouse of Venice whose bell they think they hear, and with the visit they make later in the evening to the distraught spirit they find there and his frantic lamentations over his fate. No one has really yet identified this figure and his outpourings of the miseries of rejected love, though many conjectures have been made; it has even been suggested that Shelley intended a kind of concealed autobiography. But in any case I do not think I am alone in feeling immense regret that the conversational passages, which Shelley handled so skilfully and illuminatingly, were abandoned for a style and mood far less peculiarly his own.

It is difficult not to think that the inspiration for 'Lines Written among the Euganean Hills' did not come directly from this brief sojourn with Byron in Venice. Byron's presence, Byron's conversation excited Shelley to the height of his poetic powers, and it was not long before he began what is held by many to be his supreme poetic achievement, the verse drama *Prometheus Unbound*; while Byron himself, discovering *ottava rima* in the poem of 'Beppo', and how far he could use it to express the many-sided energy of his poetic personality, abandoned what had now become the confinement of *Childe Harold*, of which he was just completing the fourth canto. In fact this meeting of the two poets in Venice can be held to have been the moment of conception of the masterpiece of each.

During Shelley's visit Byron offered him, as I have already mentioned, the Villa I Cappucini at Este, which he himself had only recently leased from Richard Hoppner, the English Consul at Venice. Shelley gladly seized this opportunity to remain near Byron with Mary, and with Claire, though her presence had to be concealed from Byron. Allegra was with them, and the arrangement was that Shelley should take

Allegra, with Elise, to Byron as soon as possible. Shelley wrote without delay to Mary urging her to join them at Este, and though her child Clara was unwell she set off at once. It was probably extremely unwise in view of Clara's condition, but one imagines that Mary felt it was all for the best that they should all be together again. When Mary and her child reached Este on 5 September, Clara at first showed signs of improvement. When Shelley, with what must seem undue impatience, decided that she was well enough to continue the journey to Venice, he hurried off ahead himself, and asked Mary to follow with Clara as soon as possible. It was a disastrous decision: soon after they reached Venice Clara's condition rapidly deteriorated, and in a few days she was dead. One cannot acquit Shelley of putting pressure on Mary to join him with the child, but one must say in his defence that he seems to have had no idea that Clara was still far from strong enough to travel. There is no doubt that Mary felt deeply wronged by the whole tragic affair, and the thought must have passed through her mind that Shelley was more interested in the fate of Allegra than in that of their own offspring.

On 5 November Shelley and Mary packed up and left I Cappucini for their travels further south. After various further stops they reached Rome on the 20th, and Shelley wrote a long letter to Peacock describing the overwhelming effect Rome had had upon him in one of the most memorable series of traveller's letters Shelley wrote to his friend.

One passage in particular is poignantly relevant:

Rome is a city, as it were, of the dead, or rather of those who cannot die, and who survive the puny generations which inhabit and pass over the spot which they have made sacred to eternity. In Rome, at least in the first enthusiasm of your recognition of ancient time, you see nothing of the Italians. The nature of the city assists the delusion, for its vast and antique walls describe a circumference of sixteen miles, and thus the population is thinly scattered over this space, nearly as great as London. Wide wild fields are enclosed within it, and there are grassy lanes and copses winding among the ruins, and a great green hill, lonely and bare, which overhangs the Tiber. The gardens of the modern palaces are like wild woods of cedars, and cypress, and pine, and the neglected walks are overgrown with weeds. The English burying-place is a green slope near the walls, under the pyramidal tomb of Cestius, and is, I think, the most beautiful and solemn cemetery I ever beheld. To see the sun shining on its bright grass, fresh, when we first visited it, with the autumnal dews, and hear the whispering of the wind among the leaves of the trees which have overgrown the tomb of Cestius, and the soil which is stirring in the sun-warm earth, and to mark the tombs, mostly of women and young people who were buried there, one might, if one were to die, desire the sleep they seem to sleep. Such is the human mind, and so it peoples with its wishes vacancy and oblivion.

It was in this English cemetery that Shelley directed that his child William should be buried; and his own ashes were placed nearby, by the direction of Trelawny, who was himself eventually buried in a plot next to it.

Surprisingly, Shelley did not write again for a month, and when he wrote, after having been in Naples for some time, he opened his letter with bitter criticism of Byron. It is difficult to understand this sudden – and violent – change of mood, and one cannot help feeling that he had been brooding on the danger of leaving Allegra in a household so recklessly conducted as the Palazzo Mocenigo, where Byron seemed so determined to indulge himself in every kind of debauchery, and to associate with the dregs of the Venetian underworld. One will never know; but the hints that Shelley gives in his letter from Naples are clear enough in their insinuations and their hardly concealed extreme anxieties about the child he had just surrendered to her father. 'He hardens himself in a kind of obstinate and self-willed folly,' he wrote to Peacock. 'He associates with wretches who seem almost to have lost the gait and physiognomy of man, and who do not scruple to avow practices which are not only not named but I believe seldom even conceived in England.' How Peacock interpreted this diatribe one cannot tell, but it would not have been surprising if he concluded, being a man of the world, that Byron had abandoned himself to orgies with prostitutes of both sexes. Shelley continues with what is almost a cry of despair:

> You may think how unwillingly I have left my little favourite Alba where she might fall again under his authority. But I have employed arguments, entreaties, everything in vain, and when these fail you know I have no longer any right. No, I do not doubt, and for his sake I ought to hope, that his present career must end up soon by some violent circumstance which must reduce our situation with respect to Alba into its ancient tie.

Remembering how happy and how intellectually stimulating Shelley's relations with Byron had been before the transfer of Allegra to Byron's care, one should perhaps conclude that Claire's laments and Mary's profound despondency after the death of little Clara, and no doubt her continuing reproaches to Shelley on that tragic occurrence, had for a time unbalanced his judgement. Also one should not forget that his health was not good at this time: he suffered from pains in his side, which may have been caused by stones in the kidneys. It must surely have been before this anti-Byron mood overwhelmed him that he wrote the 'Euganean Hills', with their unequivocal praise of Byron and the hopeful and optimistic tone in which the poem concludes. The beauty of the poetry in fact totally overrides the dark sentiments expressed in its opening passages.

Another extremely mysterious event occurred in this obscure period in Naples. A child was born on 27 December 1818, which was named Elena Adelaide Shelley, with Shelley and Mary as the registered parents. She was immediately handed over to foster-parents, perhaps in the hope of reclaiming her later, but she died eighteen months afterwards. There is nothing in Mary's letters or other writings to lead one to believe that she was the mother of this child. The story was put about by the nursemaid Elise, and Shelley's servant Paolo Foggi whom she married, that Elena was really Claire's child by Shelley, and hinted at as the truth by the Hoppners in a treacherous letter to Byron. Mary furiously denied the story, and the Foggis were dismissed; but the mystery remains. It has been suggested that the child was adopted by Shelley to compensate Mary for the loss of Clara, and Claire for the removal of Allegra from her maternal care. One can only say that in view of all the facts this interpretation seems rather far-fetched.

There is no doubt that Shelley's mood in Naples was, for most of the time, one of profound distress and despondency. As well as the 'Stanzas Written in Dejection near Naples', there are several shorter poems which are evidence of this. There is also the testimony of a young Englishman, by the name of Charles Macfarlane, otherwise unknown. He describes how he was admiring a favourite statue in the Naples Museum, when he heard an English voice close by him, also expressing admiration for the statue, and turned to see:

> an unmistakable and most interesting-looking English gentleman, in appearance not more than five or six and twenty. There was not much in the remark he had uttered, as if unconsciously; it referred to the gracefulness of the statue; it was little more than a truism or commonplace, but of that sort of commonplace which is not heard from the vulgar; and the tone of voice with which it was delivered struck me as particularly soft and touching. The speaker was very evidently in delicate health; he was very thin, and would have been very pale but for a little flush at the upper edge of the cheek; his eye was rather sunken and hollow, but at the same time uncommonly quick, brilliant and glancing; his hair was long and wavy, curling naturally; the expression of the countenance melancholy, but a melancholy frequently irradiated with liveliness and even with joyfulness. Though negligently he was neatly if not elegantly dressed. He never could have been taken for anything but a true thoroughbred English gentleman, though there were personal peculiarities about him. We fell into talk, just as if we had been old acquaintances.

MacFarlane describes how the next day they met again, made a tour of Pompeii together, and then sat on a lava rock with the sea almost washing their feet until sunset. 'My companion's expressive countenance was languid, despondent, melancholy, quite sad. He did not write them here – he certainly wrote nothing while I was with him, and was not the man to indulge in any such poetical affectations; but he *thought* here those thrilling verses which in the collection of his minor poems are called "Stanzas Written in Dejection near Naples".'

Whatever the truth may be about these weeks in Naples – and it seems unlikely that we shall ever know the full story – Shelley and Mary set forth on the last day of February 1819 on their journey from Naples back to Rome, where they arrived on 5 March, and rented rooms in a palazzo on the Corso. It is noteworthy that Shelley appears to have made no attempt to re-establish relations with Byron during this period – while he was deeply occupied with *Prometheus Unbound* and Byron with the early cantos of *Don Juan* – and in all three years passed before they came together again on the old basis. In that interval something happened in Byron's life which transformed him from the reckless and self-destroying profligate of Venice to a man who had a far firmer hold on himself and played a more acceptable rôle in the Italian society in which he mixed. Perhaps he was warned by signs of physical exhaustion in his pleasures; in any case the period in which he could with a devil-may-care ribaldry boast that 'what I get by my brains, I will spend on my b— as long as I have a tester or a t— remaining' came to an end. One evening he and an English friend went to a reception at the Contessa Benzon's, once a famous beauty. They were early, and among the other guests who soon began to appear was a young woman of fair complexion, with rosy cheeks and large eyes. She was on the arm of a man many years her senior. The Contessa Benzon prevailed on Byron to allow her to introduce him. As he bent over her hand she murmured 'La Contessa Teresa Guiccioli'. From that moment they belonged to one another; and it was not long before Byron, *more Italiano*, had become her *cavalier servente*, though when talking to his English friends he was inclined to treat such relationships, with their elaborate codes of behaviour, as slightly ridiculous. But this time it was serious, and before many weeks had passed Byron was at her side in the Guiccioli Palazzo in Ravenna, vowing eternal constancy. For once, perhaps he meant it, though the casual seductions in gondolas did not cease at once. The Count himself did not seem unduly disturbed by the growing infatuation between his pretty young wife and the handsome English peer and world-famous poet: he was wily, worldly wise and calculating, and had had enough love-life of his own not to feel the meaner pangs of jealousy. As for Byron's own friends, when they realized what had happened, most were pleased – and relieved.

Meanwhile the return to Rome was acting as an invigorating tonic to Shelley. He liked the Romans far better than other Italians he had met, he found their society stimulating and amusing, particularly in the salon of Signora Marianna Dionigi, whose *conversazioni* were among the highlights of Roman social gatherings, where distinguished foreigners were always welcome. Signora Dionigi seems to have taken particular trouble about the Shelleys, though it is true that Mary made a note in her journal one day that she was 'very old, very miserly and very mean'. Moreover she took them to hear sacred music, and went with them to the galleries.

The combination of these new friends and acquaintances and the advent of the Roman spring had a beneficial effect on Mary's spirits as well as on Shelley's health. His poetry began to pour out again. He took a particular fancy to the ruins of the Baths of Caracalla, and within a month had completed the second and third acts of *Prometheus Unbound* while ensconcing himself 'among the flowery glades, and thickets of odoriferous blossoming trees, which are extended in ever winding labyrinths among its immense platforms and dizzy arches suspended in the air'. So inspired was he by these surroundings with their mixture of the evocations of ancient Rome and the inexhaustible fertility of nature that, in his preface, he attributed the whole of the first three acts to their influence, forgetting that the first act had been written at Este. He did not write that sublime after-thought, the fourth act, until he moved to Florence in November and December 1819. In the interval he had occupied himself with a totally different work, the drama of *The Cenci*, and with translations and political poems; and, as if by chance, one of the most famous and beautiful of his lyrics, the 'Ode to the West Wind'. The vigour and versatility which he displayed in this *annus mirabilis* is all the more remarkable when one remembers that at the beginning of June his three-year-old child, the beloved 'Willmouse', had died after a short illness. Percy Florence, the one survivor of Mary's children, a great consolation to her after Willmouse's death, who in due course inherited the baronetcy when both Shelley and his father Sir Timothy were dead, was not born until 12 November.

The winter months in Florence proved too bitter for the

Shelleys, and early in the New Year of 1820 they decided to move to Pisa. They had not particularly liked the city when they made their first visit in May 1818, but it had the attraction of being the residence of Dr Vacca, who had a very high reputation as a physician and whom Shelley wished to consult about his continuing ills. An added attraction was the nearness of Maria Gisborne in Livorno. When passing through Pisa during the previous September he had also made the acquaintance of a couple known as Mr and Mrs Mason. He was in fact George William Tighe, the son of an Irish Member of Parliament, and she the Countess of Mountcashell, who as a child had been a pupil of Mary's mother, Mary Wollstonecraft. They had been living together in Pisa for some years under their assumed names. The Shelleys found them extremely sympathetic, and in their early weeks in Pisa saw a great deal of them, in fact almost every day, drawn by Mrs Mason's sense of humour, good sense and liberal opinions. Thus they began to draw a circle around them in Pisa, which was later enlarged, when Byron arrived in the autumn of 1821 and Shelley's cousin Medwin and Edward Elleker Williams and his wife Jane joined them in the famous Pisan circle.

During these months the Shelleys had little or no communication with Byron – unless letters have been lost – though Claire sent him a number of foolish letters about Allegra which he does not appear to have answered. But it was a time full of difficulties and harassments in Byron's own life. Count Guiccioli turned nasty, and demanded a separation between himself and Teresa, which the Pope eventually granted. Worse, the failure of the various political movements against the authorities, first in the Kingdom of Naples and then in the Romagna, caused the exile of Teresa's husband's family, the Gambas, from Ravenna, though it was generally held that their exile was in reality a move to get rid of Byron, whose connections with the Carbonari had been closely watched by the police. They crossed into Tuscany, and made their first stay in Florence. Third, Byron's anxiety about Allegra during all this pother, decided him to put her in a convent at Bagnacavallo. In spite of this he continued to write with great energy, finishing further cantos of *Don Juan*, and working on several poetic dramas, *Sardanapalus*, *The Two Foscari* and *Cain*, in which Tom Moore saw definite traces of the influence of Shelley. At the same time Shelley heard of the death of Keats in Rome.

It became obvious that the two poets were eager to meet again, and finally Byron wrote to Shelley from what was becoming his increasingly frustrating isolation in Ravenna. 'Could not you and I contrive to meet this summer? Could you not take a run here alone?' Shelley at first tried to persuade Byron to come to Pisa. Nothing came of that, but Byron renewed his invitation to Shelley with some urgency a few weeks later, wanting to discuss Allegra's future with him if he had to leave Ravenna for Tuscany, as now seemed inevitable. There was talk of the whole Gamba party, with Teresa and Allegra, making for Switzerland. Shelley arrived in Ravenna on the evening of 6 August, and persuaded Byron of the ill-advisedness of the Swiss scheme – which Byron was more than half persuaded of already. Byron found again all the pleasure and stimulus in Shelley's company that he had known before, and they stayed together for ten days, during which Shelley seems to have managed to persuade Byron to join him in Pisa. He wrote off to Mary as soon as Byron had agreed, and, with her usual efficiency in such matters, she set about finding a house for him at once. Eventually she took a lease for him of the large Palazzo Lanfranchi on the Lung'Arno.

Shelley wrote a comic description of the Ravenna household to Mary. Apart from the servants, he told her, there was an almost uncountable menagerie: 'Ten horses, eight enormous dogs, three monkeys, five cats, an eagle, a crow, and a falcon; and all these, except the horses, walk about the house, which every now and then resounds with their unarbitrated quarrels, as if they were the masters of it.' In a postscript he added: 'I have just met on the grand staircase five peacocks, two guinea-hens, and an Egyptian crane. I wonder who all these animals were before they were changed into these shapes.'

Byron, obedient to Teresa's demand that he cease writing *Don Juan* (which offended her taste), had written no more of it in 1821. But he read the fifth canto to Shelley while he was his guest. Shelley was overwhelmed. He wrote to Mary that 'every word has the stamp of immortality . . . It fulfils, in a certain degree, what I have long preached of producing, something wholly new and relative to the age, and yet surpassingly beautiful. It may be vanity, but I think I see the trace of my earnest exhortations to him to create something wholly new.' Cantos Three, Four and Five were published in London while Shelley was in Ravenna. As soon as copies arrived, Byron sent one to Shelley in Pisa. Shelley renewed his remarkably perceptive enthusiasm in his letter of thanks:

It is a poem totally of its own species, and my wonder and delight at the grace of the composition no less than the free and grand vigour of the conception of it perpetually increase. The few passages which anyone might desire to be cancelled in the first and second Cantos are here reduced to almost nothing. The poem carries with it at once the stamp of originality and a defiance of imitation. Nothing has ever been written like it in English – nor if I may venture to prophesy, will there be, without carrying upon it the mark of a secondary and borrowed light. You unveil and present in its true deformity what is worst in human nature, and this is what the witlings of the age murmur at, conscious of their want of power to endure the scrutiny of such a light. We are damned to the knowledge of good and evil, and it is well for us to know what we should avoid no less than what we should seek. The character of Lambro – his return – the merriment of his daughter's guests made as it were in celebration of his funeral – the meeting with the lovers – and the death of Haidée – are circumstances combined and developed in a manner that I seek elsewhere in vain. The fifth Canto, which some of your pet Zoili in Albemarle Street said was *dull*, gathers instead of loses splendour and energy – the language in which the whole is clothed – a sort of chameleon under the changing sky of the spirit that kindles it – is such as these lisping days could not have expected – and are, believe me, in spite of the approbation which you wrest from them – little pleased to hear. One can hardly judge from recitation and it was not until I read it in print that I have been able to do it justice.

Shelley was extremely modest about showing Byron his own poems. He had let him read *Prometheus Unbound*, which he had admired though perhaps not with the enthusiasm it deserved. He had also shown him, or read to him, *The Cenci*, which Byron seems to have liked though he thought it a mistake at that date to write a drama in the Jacobean manner. He had also sent him *Adonais*, but he is not on record as having discussed it with him at Ravenna, chiefly, one cannot help thinking, because Keats's work, with the exception of 'Hyperion', was unsympathetic to Byron. Shelley's own failure to find an appreciative public, when he compared it with Byron's, depressed him, but it did not in any way abate his admiration of *Don Juan*. He had no meanness of jealousy in his nature, and it was largely due to his influence with Teresa, who liked him, that she agreed, when they were all united in Pisa a few months later, to lift her ban on *Don Juan* and allow Byron to carry on with the work that was boiling up inside him.

At the same time as the Ravenna visit, Byron was vigorously occupied in a counter-attack on Southey, who in his *A Vision of Judgement*, published to celebrate the virtues of poor, mad George III, who had died at the end of January 1820, denounced what he chose to call the Satanic school of poetry, and in particular *Don Juan*, which he went so far as to call 'an act of treason in English Poetry'. This was too much for Byron to take lying down, and in the most brilliant of his satirical poems, *The Vision of Judgement*, without ill-tempered rancour and yet with deadly aim, he utterly demolished the Poet Laureate.

As soon as Shelley got back from Ravenna, with Mary's assistance he set about completing the preparations for Byron's arrival at the Palazzo Lanfranchi, and installing himself and Mary directly across the river in the Tre Palazzi di Chiesa. But Byron had a temperamental block about moving, quite apart from the fact that, with his vast assemblage of luggage, his servants and his menagerie, it was a major undertaking. He dallied and dallied, causing ceaseless anxiety to Teresa, and it was not until 1 November that the huge caravanserai arrived in Pisa.

In the course of the journey, to his surprise and over-whelming joy, he encountered a coach which contained his beloved Harrow friend, Lord Clare, whom he had not seen for seven or eight years. Clare was one of the select circle of schoolboy intimates, including Lord Delawarr and Charles David Gordon, of whom Byron was especially fond. His letters to Clare always begin 'My dearest Clare'. This unexpected meeting moved him deeply. 'It was a new and inexplicable feeling,' he wrote in his *Detached Thoughts*, 'like rising from the grave, to me. Clare, too, was much agitated – *more* in appearance than even myself; for I could feel his heart beat to his fingers' ends, unless indeed, it was the pulse of my own which made me think so . . . We were but five minutes together, and in the public road; but I hardly recollect an hour of my existence which could be weighed against them.'

They were to meet again for a day when Byron moved to the coast from Pisa; it was a meeting that left him in tears.

Another reason which recommended Pisa to the Shelleys was its proximity to Livorno, the home of Maria Gisborne and her second husband and her son by her first marriage, Henry Reveley. On the death of Mary Wollstonecraft, Maria had taken Mary Godwin into her own home, so there was already a connection of some intimacy. She appears to have been a woman of intelligence, sensible and charming, so that when they first met in Livorno in 1818, the two households became very close to each other in spite of the boringness of Gisborne himself, which Shelley described to Hogg as 'of the Erymanthian breed'. They returned to England in the spring of 1820, and in June Shelley wrote his famous letter in verse. There had been differences between the Gisbornes and Shelley, who had lent Henry Reveley some money to complete a steamboat he was at work on, but finally abandoned. Gisborne had written a very tactless letter to Shelley about this, which enraged him. However resentments never lasted long with Shelley, and there is no trace of ill-feeling in the *Letter*, in which he recalled the happy days they had spent together in Livorno and talked of his friends she would be meeting in London: Coleridge, Peacock, Leigh Hunt, Hogg and Horace Smith. It is one of his most successful light compositions, a style in which, as in the early part of *Julian and Maddolo*, he showed himself a delightful master, and makes one wish he had been able (as he intended) to write more in the same relaxed vein, so entirely different from the exalted visions of his more elaborately wrought odes and choruses, magnificent as so many of them are.

Shelley himself did not write much in the spring and summer of 1820, but was quickened by the news of the outbreak of the Greek War of Independence in the spring, brought to him by Prince Alexander Mavrocordato. This inspired him to write the lyrical drama of *Hellas*, notable among his works if only for the dazzling choruses:

> Worlds on worlds are rolling ever
>   From creation to decay,
> Like the bubbles on a river
>   Sparkling, bursting, borne away,
>   But they are still immortal
>   Who, through birth's orient portal
> And death's dark chasm hurrying to and fro,

Clothe their unceasing flight
In the brief dust and light
Gathered around their chariots as they go;
New shapes they still may weave,
New gods, new laws receive,
Bright or dim are they as the robes they last
On Death's bare ribs had cast . . .

And the triumphant opening of the final chorus:

The world's great age begins anew,
    The golden years return,
The earth doth like a snake renew
    Her winter weeds outworn:
Heaven smiles, and faiths and empires gleam,
Like wrecks of a dissolving dream . . .

With its poignant reversal in the last stanza:

Oh, cease! must hate and death return?
    Cease! must men kill and die?
Cease! drain not to its dregs the urn
    Of bitter prophecy.
The world is weary of the past,
Oh, might it die or rest at last!

Meanwhile other members of what was to become the
Pisan circle were arriving, or becoming acquainted with the
Shelleys. There was John Taaffe, a Catholic Irishman who
had been living in Pisa for several years, and whose wife had
died giving birth to the second of his two children. He was
occupied with a translation and commentary on Dante;
neither Shelley nor Byron thought much of the translation,

but were impressed by the commentary, and managed to get the first part of it published in England by Murray. He was a sincere admirer of Shelley's poetry, though Mary was inclined to find him a figure of fun. Shelley's second cousin, Tom Medwin, also arrived, an ex-soldier who had come across Shelley's poetry in India, and had immediately become a devotee. He was not a sparkling personality, and in fact to Mary was 'commonplace personified'. He came to fancy himself as Boswell to Byron, and though he lacked any outstanding gift for the rôle, his *Conversations with Lord Byron*, published in 1824, have their value, of a rather pedestrian (and not entirely reliable) sort. He became one of the group who went out practice-shooting with Byron and Shelley in the afternoons. They used to ride out to a farm in the neighbourhood and shoot at coins about the size of a half-crown tied in the cleft of a stick. Once Byron hit the coin so exactly in the middle that it folded up round his bullet. Nevertheless, and surprisingly perhaps, Shelley showed himself the best shot of the four. It was Medwin who, with his glowing talk of Shelley, persuaded a Lieutenant in the Eighth Dragoons, Edward Elleker Williams, who had sold his commission in India, and taken as his mistress an extremely attractive young woman, Jane Johnson, to join them in Pisa. The pair of them were to play a significant part in the last year of Shelley's life. Also, an old London friend of Byron's, Captain John Hay, appeared in January and settled with them in Pisa, much to Byron's pleasure. He liked to go shooting with the Gambas in the Maremma, and sent Byron presents of game - also, on one occasion, a wild boar. He appears to have been the only one of the new group of friends who did not occupy himself with any literary activities.

Finally, the most extraordinary figure of all these new friends and acquaintances, Edward John Trelawny, who had met Medwin and Williams in Switzerland in 1820, turned up in the middle of January. The magnet again was Shelley. Trelawny always had his reservations about Byron, but Shelley he all but hero-worshipped from the first moment he met him, captivated by his almost boyish charm, his ardent sincerity and the brilliance of his erudite conversation. Mary was deeply struck by him, and inclined to believe the fantastic stories he told of his earlier life. 'They are in unison,' she wrote, 'with his Moorish face (for he looks Oriental yet not Asiatic) his dark hair, his Herculean form, and there is an air of extreme good nature which pervades his whole countenance, especially when he smiles, which assures me that his heart is good.' His first encounter with Shelley is so vividly described by him that, well-known as it is, it cannot be omitted. On arrival in Pisa, he went round to the Tre Palazzi, where he dined with Edward and Jane Williams, and was soon deeply engrossed in conversation. He was suddenly put out, by seeing in the passage near the door a pair of glittering eyes steadily fixed on his, as if of an emanation emerging from the darkness. Jane saw Trelawny's astonishment, and laughingly went to the doorway saying, 'Come in Shelley, it's only our friend Tre just arrived.'

Swiftly gliding in, blushing like a girl, a tall thin stripling held out both his hands; and although I could hardly believe as I looked at his flushed, feminine artless face that it could be the Poet, I returned his warm pressure . . . Was it possible that this mild-looking, beardless boy, could be that veritable monster at war with all the world?

– excommunicated by the Fathers of the Church, deprived of his civil rights by the fiat of a grim Lord Chancellor, discarded by every member of his family, and denounced by the rival sages of our literature as the founder of a Satanic school? I could not believe it; it must be a hoax. He was habited like a boy, in a black jacket and trousers, which he seemed to have outgrown, or his tailor, as is the custom, had most shamefully stinted him in his 'sizings'.

Jane asked him what book he had with him; it turned out to be Calderón's *Mágico Prodigioso*, which he was translating. They asked him to read it to them, and:

. . . shoved off from the shore of common-place incidents that could not interest him, and fairly launched on a theme that did, he instantly became oblivious of everything but the book in his hand. The masterly manner in which he analysed the genius of the author, his lucid interpretation of the story, and the ease with which he translated into our language the most subtle and imaginative passages of the Spanish poet, were marvellous, as was his command of the two languages. After this touch of his quality I no longer doubted his identity; a dead silence ensued; looking up, I asked, 'Where is he?'

Mrs Williams said, 'Who? Shelley? Oh, he comes and goes like a spirit, no one knows when or where.'

The new group of friends made a custom of dining with Byron at the Palazzo Lanfranchi once a week, generally on a Wednesday. During these evenings they read their poems to one another, and Shelley would often launch into a subtle criticism of Byron's work. Byron had the greatest respect for Shelley's opinions on his work, and often altered – and sometimes even threw away – passages that Shelley had criticized. It was certainly in these evenings that their mutual intellectual and poetical influence was at its height. The ladies were not invited, which may seem curious to us, but was certainly accepted as normal at that time. With the ladies, however, they spent many evenings at the opera, which Mary seems to have loved as much as Shelley himself, and where Rossini was all the rage. Mary was also occupied at the time with the final stages of her new novel, *Valperga*.

Hardly had Trelawny arrived, when Shelley and Edward Williams began to make plans to spend the spring and summer boating. There is no doubt that Trelawny encouraged them, and also gave them practical advice, of which they were badly in need. Shelley's own experience of boats had only been on the Thames at home, or on the Lake of Geneva, but never on the sea. Some months before Trelawny had arrived, Shelley had already acquired, from Maria Gisborne's son Henry Reveley, a flat-bottomed boat about ten feet in length, which he had fitted with a keel, a mast and a sail. As soon as it was ready, Shelley, Williams and Reveley embarked in it for Pisa by the canal. Williams very soon showed lack of seamanship by capsizing the boat, and Reveley, luckily a good swimmer, had to help Shelley to dry land. After this inauspicious start, they had the boat reconstructed, and in the ensuing spring months spent many days sailing on the Arno or on the Serchio, sometimes venturing to the sea, with Mary or Jane (who both hated the boat) from time to time accompanying them. Shelley's fragmentary poem 'The Boat on the Serchio' is a record of these happy excursions. The poem, in which Shelley gives Williams the name of Melchior and himself Lionel, starts with a beautiful and characteristic passage:

Our boat is asleep on Serchio's stream,
Its sails are folded like thoughts in a dream,
The helm sways idly, hither and thither;
Domenic, the boatman, has brought the mast,
And the oars, and the sails; but 'tis sleeping fast,
Like a beast, unconscious of its tether.

The stars burnt out in the pale blue air,
And the thin white moon lay withering there;
To tower, and cavern, and rift, and tree,
The owl and the bat fled drowsily.
Day had kindled the dewy woods,
And the rocks above and the stream below,
And the vapours in their multitudes,
And the Appenine's shroud of summer snow,
And clothed with light of aëry gold
The mists in their eastern caverns uprolled . . .

Later in the poem, Shelley gives us a memorable and charming glimpse of boyhood reminiscence:

. . . 'Ay, heave the ballast overboard,
And stow the eatables in the aft locker.'
'Would not this keg be best a little lowered?'
'No, now's all right.' 'Those bottles of warm tea –
(Give me some straw) – must be stowed tenderly;
Such as we used, in summer after six,
To cram in greatcoat pockets, and to mix

Hard eggs and radishes and rolls at Eton,
And, couched on stolen hay in those green harbours
Farmers called gaps, and we schoolboys called arbours,
Would feast till eight . . .'

When Trelawny arrived in Pisa in January, he lost no time
in suggesting that Shelley and Williams should have a boat
built for them in which they could sail on the sea, not merely
on the rivers and canals. Knowing Williams's interest from
old days, he had brought with him the model of a schooner
which had been given him by a friend he had come to know
in Geneva but was now in Genoa, Captain Daniel Roberts,
R.N. Williams, who had begun his life as a sailor, liked the
look of it; Shelley was entranced, and wanted the boat built
at once. In Genoa Captain Roberts had access to boat-
building facilities, and Trelawny assured them he was just
the right person to entrust the job to. The plan developed:
when Trelawny saw Byron the next day, he found that he
appeared only too eager to join in. So Captain Roberts was
instructed to have two boats built: the small one for Shelley
and Williams was to be 'a small, beautiful boat about 17 or 18
feet – to be a thorough *varmint* at *pulling* and *sailing*. Single
banked oars, say four or six; and as I think, if you differ not,
three luggs and a jib – *backing ones*! She will be used for
fishing, shooting, and as a tender for the other.' Byron's
boat, however, was to be on an entirely different scale,
fitting (one supposes) his lordly rank: 'She is to have *Iron
Keel*, copper *fastenings* and *bottom* – the *Cabin* to be as *high*
and *roomy* as possible, no *expense* to be spared to make her a
complete BEAUTY! We should like to have four guns, one
on each bow, and one on each quarter, as *large* as you think
safe – to make the devil of a noise! – fitted with locks – the

swivels of brass! I suppose from one to three pounders.'
Byron was assured that she should not cost more than about
£100: in the end he found that he had spent something nearer
£1,000. But as his mother-in-law had just died, his income –
quite apart from what he earned from his poems – was more
or less doubled during the lifetime of his wife, and thriftier
and thriftier though he was becoming, the expenditure
doesn't seem to have worried him overmuch.

The spring came early in Pisa in 1822. Apart from the
pleasures of boating (during which Mary and Jane seemed
rather to experience the mishaps) and the afternoons spent in
pistol-practice in the farm outside the city limits, they took
long walks in the pine forests along the shore, Shelley and
Jane being most frequently together. Jane had, it seems,
hypnotic powers, and began to put Shelley under to relieve
the constant pains he suffered in his side. Her musical talents
also formed a great attraction for him, and he presented her
with a guitar. Out of their musical hours together, these
hypnotic sessions and their walks along the seashore, came a
group of Shelley's most attractive lyrics which, with their
simplicity and their songlike purity, show an almost
unmistakable influence of Byron's more spontaneous lyrics.
It is difficult to believe that he would have written such lyrics
without the poetic cross-fertilization that was a feature of
their relationship at this time. But it would, I think, be a
mistake to think that such exquisite poems as 'With a
Guitar', 'To Jane', 'Lines Written in the Bay of Lerici' (with
its deliberate reference to Edward Williams as Prince
Ferdinand to Jane's Miranda), or 'To Jane: The Invitation'
and 'To Jane: The Recollection' (which were originally
drafted as one poem called 'The Pine Forest of the Cascini
near Pisa') denote that Shelley had conceived for Jane a new

infatuation, such as he had had for Emilia Viviani. Volatile though his emotions were, Mary had been with Jane and Shelley on one of the famous seaside walks, and certainly Shelley showed 'The Bay of Lerici' to Williams, and even asked his opinion whether Jane should be allowed to read it. It seems unlikely, to say the least, that as they all lived together in the same house Mary should not have seen these poems.

The reference to himself as 'the serpent' in his poem 'To Edward Williams', went back to a joke of Byron's: 'Goethe's Mephistopheles calls the serpent who tempted Eve, "My Aunt, the renowned Snake", and I always insist that Shelley is nothing but one of her nephews walking about on the tip of his tail.' Whether the joke implied that Shelley had the habit of gliding about the house noiselessly – as Trelawny's description might suggest – or was a reference to his atheism, we do not know. Shelley in any case took it in good part, as he took his old friend Peacock's comic portrait of him as Scythrop in *Nightmare Abbey* in good part. He had more sense of humour than some of those who have attempted to portray him have given him credit for. 'Alas, poor Shelley,' Byron observed after his death, 'how he would have laughed had he lived, and how we used to laugh now and then at various things that are grave in the suburbs.'

These idyllic weeks in Pisa during the winter and early spring in 1821–22 were certainly one of the happiest periods in Shelley's life, and perhaps of Byron's too. Apart from his shorter lyrics, Shelley was engaged on a play about Charles I, which was never finished, and Byron, once Teresa's interdict had been lifted, on further cantos of *Don Juan*. He had his mistress with him, her brother Pietro of whom he was extremely fond, and only a few yards away across the river, a circle of intelligent, convivial and admiring friends, all deep in literary pursuits, and regular shooting-practice at the farm belonging to a friend of Dr Vacca's in the nearby countryside. They dined with one another in the evenings, with the special Wednesday stag-parties reserved for the Palazzo Lanfranchi, and visited the opera as often as they could. Byron rarely accompanied them, as he thoroughly disliked being stared at – through opera-glasses – by the audience. One day in February Byron suggested that they should produce *Othello* in the great hall of the Palazzo Lanfranchi. He proposed himself as Iago, Trelawny as Othello, Williams as Cassio and Medwin as Roderigo; Mary was to take the part of Desdemona, and Jane of Emilia. Shelley was not given a part, nor Teresa owing to the difficulty she would have in memorizing English lines. In any case it was finally dropped, in spite of the enthusiasm for the project which reigned for some days. It seems that Teresa was the cause: perhaps she did not like the idea of Byron simulating interest in other women, or perhaps the atmosphere of violent passion engendered by the play disturbed her. Her disapproval did not show her in her best light, but the very existence of the proposal indicated how intimate the relations between the members of the English circle had become.

This industrious, creative calm was interrupted towards the end of March by an incident which looked for a time as if it might cause serious trouble to them all. The full facts, together with all the correspondence it involved between Byron, Shelley, Taaffe, the British Consul, Dawkins, and the Tuscan authorities are given in Professor Clarence Cline's *Byron, Shelley and their Pisan Circle*. The usual cavalcade was returning to Florence one afternoon from their regular shooting-practice at the farm, with the front row of horses, Taaffe, Byron, Shelley and Trelawny strung out across the road. Captain Hay and Pietro Gamba formed a second line just behind them. Williams had not joined the party, and Medwin had already left Pisa. About a quarter of a mile from the Piagge Gate, another rider galloped up behind them and endeavoured to pass them in the narrow space between the front line and the ditch. In doing so he brushed Taaffe's horse, which reared and bumped into Byron's horse. 'Have you ever seen the like of that?' exclaimed Taaffe. Shelley immediately galloped off in pursuit, followed by Byron and Trelawny.

It is difficult not to think that the Englishmen made too much fuss of the incident, which was really caused by the fact that the horseman, Sergeant-Major Masi of the Tuscan Royal Light Horse, was in a great hurry not to be late for roll-call, and that the Englishmen were in fact occupying the greater part of the road. Unfortunately Byron, deluded by the gaudiness of the Sergeant-Major's uniform and his epaulettes, assumed he was an officer and, galloping in pursuit of him, offered him his card, meaning that he was challenging him to a duel. Once that mistake had been made, the lamentable results were almost bound to follow. After some heated argument, Masi lost his temper and everyone began to slash at everyone else with drawn sabres. Shelley was knocked from his horse by a blow on the back of his head, and Hay was cut on the nose: the wound bled profusely. Teresa and Mary were in a carriage in which they had driven out to meet their men-friends on their return. Seeing the affray, they turned back and drove as fast as they could to the Palazzo Lanfranchi, Teresa as usual almost in convulsions and Mary trying to calm her. Further outbreaks of angry altercation followed in the now crowded streets, and then Masi galloped off. As he passed the Palazzo in the narrow roadway, a man in Byron's livery struck at him with a lance, and wounded him in the side. It was this attack which made the whole affair much more serious than it might otherwise have been. The first rumours were that Masi was not expected to live through the night, while in the Palazzo Captain Hay had still not had his wound properly attended to. At last an English physician, Dr John Todd, was found to look after him, while Byron sent out orders that Masi was to be seen to at his expense. Hearing the rumours of Masi's plight, the English party despatched their account of the affray to the Italian authorities as soon as possible, and also to the English Consul in Florence; for if Masi died they might easily be accused of murder. After five or six days, however, Masi's condition improved to the point where he could be considered out of danger. Though it was never officially admitted, there can be little doubt that it was Byron's coachman, Papi, who was responsible for the wounding.

Taaffe seems to have played a far from glorious part in the affair, for which he was nicknamed by Jane 'False Taaffe' or in fact 'Falstaff'. It was he who started the whole thing off by his exclamation when Masi brushed past him, but he did not follow the others in pursuit. His hat was knocked off in the mêlée, and for fear that he should be thought to have fallen off his horse – he was extremely sensitive about his horsemanship – asked a passing peasant woman to pick it up for him. While he was brushing the dust off it, the encounter at the Piagge Gate was taking place, so that he arrived late on the scene and was able to disclaim any involvement. His attempt to exculpate himself in this fashion caused great annoyance to Byron and the others; it seemed to them rather craven, and his behaviour in their eyes was not improved by the fact that, without consultation with them, he called on Masi's Commander, Captain Chiesi, requesting a guarantee that the Englishmen should be protected from any retaliatory action by Masi's fellow soldiers. Taaffe got the answer he deserved: that the Captain's troop was too honourable to contemplate such an action.

If they had known of it at the time, the others would have found Taaffe's behaviour even more despicable for the letter he took upon himself to send to Dawkins on Wednesday night, 27 March, in which he wrote:

Not considering myself any way more implicated than as a casual spectator of part of the fray, I should not have thought it necessary to trouble you about it, were it not that his Lordship tells me he sent you a note of mine; by which it appears he has used my name as freely as he chose. I must then tell you that when I come to be juridically examined my oath must be the enclosed. You will thus see that in fact I was but a spectator of an inconsiderable part of the business and a real actor in none of it . . . Lord Byron is not accused of striking the man neither did he receive any sabre blows – so that except he used hard words or gave or accepted a challenge he might consider himself as little engaged otherwise than juridically on account of the stab supposed given by one of his servants; and herein his innocence will be proved . . . But as to me, I certainly disclaim any participation where I might have trouble and vexation without end without the possibility of gaining any credit . . .

In the end, Byron generously forgave Taaffe, though there is no further mention of him in the comings and goings of the English group. The whole business might easily have turned out to be a considerable embarrassment to Byron, as he was already under close watch by the Tuscan police. In fact, if Masi had not recovered there is no knowing where the repercussions might have ended.

In the midst of all this, a more personal disaster occurred in Byron's life, in the sudden death of Allegra in the convent at Bagnacavallo. That he was deeply distressed by this misfortune is certain, and yet he showed little of his feelings outwardly at the time. 'The blow was stunning and unexpected,' he wrote to Shelley on hearing the news, 'but I have borne up against it as I best can, and so far successfully, that I can go about the usual business of life with the same appearance of composure, and even greater.' One almost gets the impression that Shelley was more deeply affected than Byron. He had the disagreeable task of breaking the news to Claire, who was stunned with horror, but did not break down as they thought she might. She asked to be given permission to see the coffin before it was sent to England as Byron intended. She also asked for a picture of her and a lock of her hair, both of which Byron sent her. In the end she was persuaded by the Shelleys not to visit the coffin when it was embarked for England at Livorno.

Not many days later, Shelley had one of his visions or hallucinations, which was clearly brought about by Allegra's death. He went for a moonlight walk with Williams by the shore, when, as Williams wrote in his diary:

He grasped me violently by the arm and stared steadfastly on the white surf that broke upon the beach under our feet. Observing him sensibly affected, I demanded of him if he was in pain – but he only answered, saying 'There it is again! There!' He recovered after some time, and declared that he saw, as plainly as then he saw me, a naked child rise from the sea, clap its hands as if in joy, and smiling at him. This was a trance that it required some reasoning and philosophy entirely to awaken him from, so forcibly had the vision operated on his mind.

Byron's plan was to have Allegra buried in the church at Harrow, plainly describing her as the 'daughter of G.G. Lord Byron'. Almost unbelievable as it may seem to us today, this plan was prevented by the horrified prudery of the churchwardens and parishioners, and in the end poor Allegra was buried in the church porch, without any tablet or memorial.

As summer approached, Byron and his English friends decided that they must leave the stifling heat of Pisa for houses nearer the sea and the sea-breezes. Byron chose a house a few miles south of Livorno, the Villa Dupuy in Montenegro, with a fine view of the sea and a garden which was soon full of the scent of flowers. He took advantage of its closeness to Livorno to visit the Mediterranean squadron of the United States fleet, which happened to be at anchor there. He was received with the greatest friendliness and honour, and his dreams of emigrating to America were reawakened. Meanwhile the Shelleys began a long and frustrating search for a suitable house, not too near to Byron because Claire was still in the offing, but as near the sea as possible. Finally, at the end of April, they had to settle for the Casa Magni at San Terenzo, not far from Lerici. It was far from ideal, because they had to share it with the Williamses as well as Claire at the beginning, and their quarters were cramped. Also Mary found the villagers who lived in the neighbourhood extremely wild, almost savage, and neither she nor Jane was happy there. She was also feeling far from well. Godwin, the eternal sponger, had once more renewed his demands on Shelley to pay his debts. For Shelley and Williams, however, all troubles and inconveniences were swallowed up by the arrival of their newly built boat at Lerici on 12 May. They were delighted as children with a new toy. 'The boat sailed like a witch,' Shelley wrote to Roberts. 'She is a most beautiful boat, and so far surpasses both mine and Williams's expectations that it was with some difficulty that we could persuade ourselves that you had not sent us the *Bolivar* [the name Byron had finally chosen for his own boat, which did not arrive for another month] by mistake.' They immediately started to try her out, but on their earliest expeditions found that she was too light and needed two tons of pig-iron to bring her down to her bearings; nor did she behave well in a breeze. This was serious, though they did not discover how serious for some time. What was more embarrassing to all of them was that the name *Don Juan* was painted in large black letters on the sail, making her look, as Mary sourly observed, 'like a coal barge'. Eventually they had to cut out the piece of sail with the offending letters on it, and substitute another plain piece of sail. She was then renamed the *Ariel*, and when Trelawny arrived in June he found both Shelley and Williams in ecstasy over her, even dreaming of trying her out on the Atlantic. Williams was becoming a capable sailor, but Shelley still stuck to his belief that he could steer with one hand and read, holding a volume of Plato with the other at the same time. Trelawny was sceptical, and anxious. Mary, though she was three months pregnant and in poor spirits, went out with them sometimes, but one cannot escape the impression that she had an unhappy and only half-conscious sense of foreboding the whole time.

In the early summer of 1822 Shelley seems to have abandoned his drama on Charles I, under the strong feeling, which was not jealousy, that in comparison with Byron his poetry was getting him nowhere – or nowhere he wanted to go. In a letter to Horace Smith he wrote despondently: 'I do not write – I have lived too long near Lord Byron and the sun has extinguished the glowworm.' In saying this he was not being quite truthful. He had in fact started a long poem which, if he had lived to finish it, might have turned out to be one of his chief mature masterpieces. In its incomplete form 'The Triumph of Life', consisting of over 500 lines in *terza rima*, was first published by Mary Shelley in her edition of his *Posthumous Poems* of 1824. Since 1816, when he and Byron had read *La Nouvelle Héloïse* together at Geneva, Shelley had become even more deeply interested in Rousseau, and cast him for a leading rôle in the new poem. It seems probable that he had been brought to the idea of writing a Dante-esque poem, though in Petrarchan form resembling Petrarch's *Trionfi*, by reading Byron's *The Prophecy of Dante*. Rousseau was to play as it were the part of Virgil in Dante's great poem, interpreting for the poet a symbolic and terrible vision of the modern world which unrolls before them; though the poem was, it seems fairly clear, not to have the implications of revolutionary action that Byron had given *The Prophecy of Dante*, but rather an exposition of the Platonic ideal of the life of contemplation, of thought and moral values, to which Shelley had been increasingly drawn, as one can see in his immediately preceding work, and in the *Defence of Poetry*. One of my chief regrets about Shelley's early death is that he did not live to work out, in the extraordinary and powerful imagery he was employing, the full implications of these countervailing ideas. One cannot, of course, do more than conjecture where the conclusion of what was obviously intended as a very long poem would have arrived. What we have is a kind of *Inferno*, in which the disillusionments and horrors of life are mercilessly displayed, as the Triumphal Car, driven onwards by its Janus-faced charioteer with bandaged eyes, sweeps on, crushing all in its path, emperors, kings, priests, conquerors as well as the host of ordinary deluded mortals, all except 'the sacred few . . . of Athens or Jerusalem' (and here surely he means us to think of Socrates and Christ), escaping its ruthless progress. Remembering the transformation that brings *Prometheus Unbound* to an optimistic end, it is not unreasonable to believe that a concluding section, as in the *Trionfi*, would have given voice to a more hopeful vision of man's destiny that Shelley never, in his darkest moments, entirely abandoned.

For this new poem he used the *terza rima* form, which he had already used in the 'Ode to the West Wind', though that poem should rather be described as a sequence of *terza rima* sonnets.

The poem-fragment breaks off with an outburst, whether by Rousseau or the poet one cannot be quite certain, mysterious and tantalizing: '"Then what is life?" I cried . . .'

Towards the end of June Mary had a miscarriage and might easily have died had it not been for the presence of mind of Shelley in making her sit in ice. Though Shelley himself seemed in high spirits, he had a recurrence of his nightmare hallucinations, which thoroughly alarmed Mary in her low-spirited state following the miscarriage. On one occasion he rushed screaming into Mary's room in the middle of the night, and went on screaming until she fled from the room and flung herself at the door of the Williamses' room. When he came to – or woke up – he said he had had two visions – or dreams: in the first of which Edward and Jane had appeared to him, mangled and battered, and told him that the sea was pouring into the house and reducing it to ruins; in the second that he was strangling Mary.

At long last the arrival in Italy of Leigh Hunt and his family was signalled. They had sailed from London originally in mid-November, but violently stormy weather had made them put into port on the south coast several times. They did not arrive in Genoa until early June 1822. From there Hunt wrote to Shelley, telling him they intended to proceed to Livorno in the same ship, arriving at about the end of June. Shelley wrote welcoming him with enthusiasm, and told him that the ground floor of the Palazzo Lanfranchi was being prepared for him and his family.

It was Byron, having reason to be grateful to Hunt for sympathetic reviews in the *Examiner*, who had first of all suggested to Shelley, when he arrived in Pisa, that Hunt should be invited to join them in Italy, and produce with them a periodical to be called the *Liberal*. He was after all an experienced editor and his political views were identified with theirs. Byron had in fact originally suggested the idea to Shelley in Venice, but only in the most tentative way. Shelley now wrote off to Hunt from Pisa, urging him to accept Byron's proposal:

He proposes that you should come and go shares with him and me, in a periodical work, to be conducted here; in which each of the contracting parties should publish all their original compositions, and share the profits. He proposed it to Moore, but for some reason it was never brought to bear. There can be no doubt that the profits of any scheme in which you and Lord Byron engage, must, from various yet cooperating reasons, be very great. As to myself, I am, for the present, only a sort of link between you and him, until you can know each other and effectuate the arrangement; since (to entrust you with a secret which, for your sake, I withheld from Lord Byron), nothing would induce me to share in the profits, and still less in the borrowed splendour, of such a partnership.

Hunt wrote at first refusing, but a fortnight later changed his mind, and prepared to sail. Shelley sent him £150 (less £30 which he wisely held in reserve), but Hunt, in a typically tactless letter, asked Byron for a further 'loan' of £250, to which Byron agreed. Little did he know (or could have known at that stage) what he was letting himself in for.

As soon as Shelley knew for certain that Hunt was about to reach Livorno he sailed down to meet him in the *Don Juan* with Williams and Captain Roberts, and after a tiresome night's delay due to the closing of the health office, took him up to Byron's villa at Montenegro. It so happened that at that very moment a drama was taking place there, which must have bewildered and astonished the Hunts as an introduction to life in Italy. The coachman Papi (the real culprit in the Masi affair) had gone berserk after being told to fetch water for the household from a spring. He started declaiming wildly against the rich, and threatening anyone who attempted to leave the house. In the course of the uproar Count Pietro went out to try and calm Papi and the now thoroughly excited servants, and received a knife-wound, luckily not serious, in the arm. Byron took the incident with his usual coolness, and tried to set out for his afternoon ride, in spite of the fury of Pietro and the inevitable hysterics of his sister Teresa. When he emerged from the house, he found that Papi's mood had changed with the suddenness of a sea-squall: he flung himself down, burst into tears, and begged for forgiveness. Byron told him that he was forgiven, but also told him that he must leave his service. The police, for whom Fletcher had been sent, would in any case, it is certain, have insisted.

It was an inopportune moment for the Hunts to arrive, but what made it even more awkward was that the Tuscan authorities had just decided to exile the Gamba family from their territory. Byron – and some of his friends – believed that the move was really aimed at him, though the British Consul did not agree. In any case their suspicions about the Masi case were not completely allayed, and the appearance of the *Bolivar*, with its two cannons mounted on board, inflamed these suspicions again. It is not surprising, therefore, that Byron was in a bad mood. But a far worse misfortune was about to overwhelm them all.

Shelley took the Hunts to Pisa, showed them the sights, and then introduced them to their new quarters in the Palazzo Lanfranchi, to which Byron and Teresa followed. These courtesies completed, he hurried back to Livorno, where Williams was waiting impatiently to sail for San Terenzo and home.

The weather was hot and thundery that afternoon.

Captain Roberts did not like the look of it, and wanted them to wait until the following morning. The wind was, however, fair for Lerici, and both Williams and Shelley decided they would take advantage of it, and set off with the eighteen-year-old sailor-boy Charles Vivian soon after one o'clock. Trelawny had intended to take the *Bolivar* with them, but the port authorities prevented him as he had not yet got his clearance papers. Captain Roberts walked out to the end of the mole to keep an uneasy eye on the *Don Juan* as long as she was visible. Trelawny's Genoese mate sensed that a squall was coming up and noted that the *Don Juan* was steering a course too close inshore and carrying too much sail. At about three o'clock Roberts saw the squall approaching the bay, and went up into the watch-tower to keep the *Don Juan* in view as long as possible: she was then about ten miles out to sea, and was taking in sail. Trelawny on the *Bolivar* had lost sight of her, and went down to his cabin to take a nap. He has left a graphic account of what followed:

I was roused by a noise over-head and went on deck. The men were getting up a chain cable to let go another anchor. There was a general stir amongst the shipping; shifting berths, getting down yards and masts, veering out cables, hauling in of hawsers, letting go anchors, hailing from the ships and quays, boats sculling rapidly to and fro. It was almost dark, although only half-past six o'clock. The sea was of the colour, and looked as solid and smooth as a sheet of lead, and covered with an oily scum. Gusts of wind swept over without ruffling it, and big drops of rain fell on its surface, rebounding, as if they could not penetrate it. There was a commotion in the air, made up of many threatening sounds, coming upon us from the sea. Fishing-craft and coasting-vessels under bare poles rushed by us in shoals, running foul of the ships in the harbour. As yet the din and hubbub was that made by men but their shrill pipings were suddenly silenced by the crashing voice of a thunder squall that burst right over our heads. For some time no other sounds were to be heard than the thunder, wind, and rain. When the fury of the storm, which did not last for more than twenty minutes, had abated, and the horizon was in some degree cleared, I looked to seaward anxiously, in the hope of descrying Shelley's boat, amongst the many small craft scattered about. I watched every speck that loomed on the horizon, thinking that they would have borne up on their return to the port, as all the other boats that had gone out in the same direction had done.

I sent our Genoese mate on board some of the returning craft to make inquiries, but they all professed not to have seen the English boat . . . I did not leave the *Bolivar* until dark. During the night it was gusty and showery, and the lightning flashed along the coast: at daylight I returned on board, and resumed my examination of the crews of the various boats which had returned to port during the night. They either knew nothing, or would say nothing. My Genoese, with the quick eye of a sailor, pointed out, on board a fishing-boat, an English-made oar, that he thought he had seen in Shelley's boat, but the entire crew swore by all the saints in the calendar that this was not so. Another day was passed in horrid suspense. On the morning of the third day I rode to Pisa. Byron had returned to the Lanfranchi Palace. I hoped to find a letter from the Villa Magni: there was none. I told my fears to

Hunt, and then went upstairs to Byron. When I told him, his lip quivered, and his voice faltered as he questioned me . . . On my arrival at Via Reggio I heard that a punt, a water-keg, and some bottles had been found on the beach. These things I recognised as having been in Shelley's boat when he left Leghorn . . . It was not until many days after this that my worst fears were confirmed. Two bodies were found on the shore, one near Via Reggio, which I went and examined. The face and hands, and parts of the body not protected by the dress were fleshless. The tall slight figure, the jacket, the volume of Sophocles in one pocket, and Keats's poems in the other, doubled back, as if the reader, in the act of reading, had hastily thrust it away, were all too familiar to me to leave a doubt in my mind that this mutilated corpse was any other than Shelley's. The other body was washed on shore three miles distant from Shelley's, near the tower of Migliarino, at the Bocca Lericcio. I went there at once. This corpse was much more mutilated; it had no other covering than – the shreds of a shirt, and that partly drawn over the head, as if the wearer had been in the act of taking it off – a black silk handkerchief, tied sailor-fashion around the neck – socks – and one boot, indicating also that he had attempted to strip. The flesh, sinews, and muscles hung about in rags, like the shirt, exposing the ribs and bones. I had brought with me from Shelley's house a boot of Williams's, and this exactly matched the one the corpse had on . . . I mounted my horse, and rode to the Gulf of Spezia, put up my horse, and walked until I caught sight of the lone house on the sea-shore in which Shelley and Williams had dwelt, and where their widows still lived. Hitherto in my frequent visits – in the absence of direct evidence to the contrary – I had buoyed up their spirits by maintaining that it was not impossible but that the friends still lived; now I had to extinguish the last hope of these forlorn women . . . I went up the stairs, and, un-announced, entered the room. I neither spoke, nor did they question me. Mrs Shelley's large grey eyes were fixed on my face. I turned away. Unable to bear this horrid silence, with a convulsive effort she exclaimed – 'Is there no hope?'

I did not answer, but left the room, and sent the servant with the children to them . . .

What Trelawny does not say in this account of the terrible moment, is that a few minutes later he returned to the room and, instead of attempting any kind of consolation, launched into a passionate eulogy of Shelley. For this Mary was undyingly grateful.

There now remained the almost all too painful problem of the disposal of the bodies. Trelawny took charge, and arranged everything, with the assistance of the British Consul, Dawkins. Owing to the strict enforcement of the quarantine laws of the two states involved – Tuscany and Lucca, and the Papal States in addition if Shelley's remains were, as he had wished, to be placed in the Protestant Cemetery in Rome – the bodies had been buried in quicklime just where they had been found on the shore. Through Dawkins, Trelawny obtained permission to have the bodies burned where they lay in the quicklime, and to transport the ashes wherever it was decided thereafter.

Trelawny's *Recollections* continue:

I got a furnace made at Leghorn, of iron-bars and strong

sheet-iron, supported on a stand, and laid in a stock of fuel, and such things as were said to be used by Shelley's much loved Hellenes on their funeral pyres.

On August 13, 1882, I went on board the *Bolivar*, with an English acquaintance, having written to Byron and Hunt to say I would send them word when everything was ready, as they wished to be present. I had previously engaged two large feluccas, with drags and tackling, to go before, and endeavour to find the place where Shelley's boat had foundered; the captain of one of the feluccas having asserted that he was out in the fatal squall, and had seen Shelley's boat go down off Via Reggio, with all sail set. With light and fitful breezes we were eleven hours reaching our destination – the tower of Migliarino, at the Bocca Lericcio, in the Tuscan States. There was a village there, and about two miles from that place Williams was buried. So I anchored, landed, called on the officer in command, a major, and told him my object in coming, of which he was already apprised by his own government. He assured me I should have every aid from him. As it was too late in the day to commence operations, we went to the only inn in the place, and wrote to Byron to be with us next day at noon. The major sent my letter to Pisa by a dragoon, and made arrangements for the next day. In the morning he was with us early, and gave me a note from Byron, to say he would join us as near noon as he could. At ten we went on board the commandant's boat, with a squad of soldiers in working dresses, armed with mattocks and spades, an officer of the quarantine service, and some of his crew. They had their peculiar tools, so fashioned as to do their work without coming into personal contact with things that might be infectious –

long handled tongs, nippers, poles with iron hooks and spikes, and divers others that gave one a lively idea of the implements of torture devised by the holy inquisitors. Thus freighted, we started, my own boat following with the furnace, and the things I had brought from Leghorn. We pulled along the shore for some distance, and landed at a line of strong posts and railings which projected into the sea – forming the boundary dividing the Tuscan and Lucchese States. We walked along the shore, where Byron and Hunt soon joined us: they, too, had an officer and soldiers from the tower of Migliarino, an officer of the Health Office, and some dismounted dragoons, so we were surrounded by soldiers, but they kept the ground clear, and readily lent their aid. There was a considerable gathering of spectators from the neighbourhood, and many ladies richly dressed were amongst them. The spot where the body lay was marked by the gnarled root of a pine tree.

A rude hut, built of young pine-tree stems, and wattled with their branches, to keep the sun and rain out, and thatched with reeds, stood on the beach to shelter the look-out man on duty. A few yards from this was the grave, which we commenced opening – the Gulf of Spezia and Leghorn at equal distances of twenty-two miles from us. As to fuel I might have saved myself the trouble of bringing any, for there was an ample supply of broken spars and planks cast on the shore from wrecks, besides the fallen and decaying timber in a stunted pine forest close at hand. The soldiers collected fuel whilst I erected the furnace, and then the men of the Health Office set to work, shovelling away the sand which covered the body, while we gathered round, watching anxiously. The first indication of their having found the body, was the appearance of the end of a black silk handkerchief – I grabbed this out with a stick, for we were not allowed to touch anything with our hands – then some shreds of linen were met with, and a boot with the bone of the leg and the foot in it. On the removal of a layer of brush-wood, all that now remained of my lost friend was exposed – a shapeless mass of bones and flesh. The limbs separated from the trunk on being touched.

'Is that a human body?' exclaimed Byron. 'Why it's more like the carcase of a sheep, or any other animal, than a man: this is a satire on our pride and folly.'

I pointed to the letters E.E.W. on the black silk handkerchief.

Byron looking on, muttered, 'The entrails of a worm hold together longer than the potter's clay, of which man is made. Hold! let me see the jaw,' he added, as they were removing the skull, 'I recognise anyone by the teeth, with whom I have talked. I always watch the lips and mouth: they tell what the tongue and eyes try to conceal.'

I had a boot of Williams's with me: it exactly corres-ponded with the one found in the grave. The remains were removed piecemeal into the furnace.

'Don't repeat this with me,' said Byron, 'let my carcase rot where it falls.'

The funeral pyre was now ready; I applied the fire, and the materials being dry and resinous the pine-wood burnt furiously, and drove us back. It was hot enough before, there was no breath of air, and the loose sand scorched our feet. As soon as the flames became clear, and allowed us to approach, we threw frankincense and salt into the furnace, and poured a flask of wine and oil over the body.

The Greek oration was omitted, for we had lost our Hellenic bard. It was now so insufferably hot that the officers and soldiers were all seeking shade.

'Let us try the strength of these waters that drowned our friends,' said Byron, with his usual audacity. 'How far out do you think they were when their boat sank?'

'If you don't wish to be put into the furnace, you had better not try; you are not in condition.'

He stripped, and went into the water, and so did I and my companion. Before we got a mile out, Byron was sick, and persuaded to return to the shore. My companion, too, was seized with cramp, and reached the land by my aid. At four o'clock the funeral pyre burnt low, and when we uncovered the furnace, nothing remained in it but dark-coloured ashes, with fragments of the larger bones. Poles were now put under the red-hot furnace, and it was gradually cooled in the sea. I gathered together the human ashes, and placed them in a small oak-box, bearing an inscription on a brass plate, screwed it down, and placed it in Byron's carriage. He returned with Hunt to Pisa, promising to be with us on the following day at Via Reggio (Aug. 16th). I returned with my party the same way we came, and supped and slept at the inn. On the following morning we went on board the same boats, with the same things and party, and rowed down the little river near Via Reggio to the sea, pulled along the coast towards Massa, then landed, and began our preparations as before.

Three white wands had been stuck in the sand to mark the Poet's grave, but as they were some distance from each other, we had to cut a trench thirty yards in length, in the line of the sticks, to ascertain the exact spot, and it was nearly an hour before we came on the grave.

In the meantime Byron and Leigh Hunt arrived in the carriage, attended by soldiers, and the Health Officer, as before . . . As I thought of the delight Shelley felt in such scenes of loneliness and grandeur whilst living, I felt we were no better than a herd of wolves or a pack of wild dogs, in tearing out his battered and naked body from the pure yellow sand that lay so lightly over it, to drag him back to the light of day; but the dead have no voice, nor had I power to check the sacrilege – the work went on silently in the deep and unresisting sand, not a word was spoken, for the Italians have a touch of sentiment, and their feelings are easily excited into sympathy. Even Byron was silent and thoughtful. We were startled and drawn together by a dull hollow sound that followed the blow of a mattock; the iron had struck a skull, and the body was soon uncovered. Lime had been strewn on it; this, or decomposition, had the effect of staining it of a dark and ghastly indigo colour. Byron asked me to preserve the skull for him; but remembering that he had formerly used one as a drinking-cup, I was determined Shelley's should not be so profaned. The limbs did not separate from the trunk, as in the case of Williams's body, so the corpse was removed entire into the furnace. I had taken the precaution of having more and longer pieces of timber, in consequence of my experience of the day before of the difficulty of consuming a corpse in the open air with our apparatus. After the fire was well kindled we repeated the ceremony of the previous day; and more wine was poured over Shelley's body than he had consumed during his life. This with the oil and salt made the yellow flames glisten and quiver. The heat from the sun and fire was so intense that the atmosphere was tremulous and wavy. The corpse fell open and the heart was laid bare. The frontal bone of the skull, where it had been struck with the mattock, fell off; and, as the back of the head had rested on the red-hot bottom bars of the furnace, the brains literally seethed, bubbled and boiled as in a cauldron, for a very long time.

Byron could not face this scene, he withdrew to the beach and swam off to the *Bolivar*. Leigh Hunt remained in the carriage. The fire was so fierce as to produce a white heat on the iron, and to reduce its contents to grey ashes. The only portions that were not consumed were some fragments of bones, the jaw, and the skull, but what surprised us all, was that the heart remained entire. In snatching this relic from the fiery furnace, my hand was severely burnt; and had anyone seen me do that act I should have been put into quarantine.

After cooling the iron machine in the sea, I collected the human ashes and placed them in a box, which I took on board the *Bolivar*. Byron and Hunt retraced their steps to their home, and the officers and soldiers returned to their quarters. I liberally rewarded the men for the admirable manner in which they behaved during the two days they had been with us.

Byron sent his own brief account of the ghastly episode in a letter to Moore towards the end of the month.

The other day at Via Reggio, I thought it proper to swim off to my schooner (the *Bolivar*) in the offing, and thence to shore again – about three miles, or better, in all. As it was at mid-day, under a boiling sun, the consequence has been a feverish attack, and my whole skin's coming off, after going through the process of one large continuous blister, raised by the sun and the sea together. I have suffered much pain; not being able to lie on my back, or even side; for my shoulders and arms were equally St Bartholomewed. But it is over – and I have got a new skin, and am as glossy as a snake in its new suit.

We have been burning the bodies of Shelley and Williams on the sea-shore, to render them fit for removal and regular interment. You can have no idea what an extraordinary effect such a funeral pile has, on a desolate mountain shore, with mountains in the back-ground and the sea before, and the singular appearance the salt and frankincense gave to the flame. All of Shelley was consumed, except the *heart*, which would not take the flame, and is now preserved in spirits of wine.

There is no doubt that Byron was deeply affected by Shelley's death, even in the midst of his worries about moving from Tuscany and the difficult situation of Teresa and the Gambas which resulted from it. In addition, he found himself landed with the problem of Leigh Hunt and the *Liberal*, and though he did not lose his respect and affection for Hunt himself, Mrs Hunt and the younger children were a sore trial in the Palazzo Lanfranchi. He thought these children behaved like 'little Yahoos', messing up the walls with their grimy fingers, and he seems to have been quite right. Mrs Hunt, however, who was determined not to be overawed, in her invertedly snobbish reaction, by a noble lord, made an entry in her diary which leaves one almost speechless by its self-righteous insensitivity: 'Mr Hunt was much annoyed by Lord Byron behaving so meanly about the children disfiguring his house which his nobleship chose to be very severe upon. Can anything be more absurd than a peer of the realm – and a *poet* making such a fuss about three or four children disfiguring the walls of a few rooms – the very children would flush for him, fye Lord B – fye.'

Trelawny records that on one occasion when Byron was leaving his rooms on the first floor, he said to his bulldog Moretto, who was always kept on guard on a long chain outside, 'Don't let any Cockneys pass this way.' And patted him on the head.

In a letter to Murray, before the cremation, Byron wrote: '. . .You are all brutally mistaken about Shelley who was without exception – the *best* and least selfish man I ever knew. I never knew one who was not a beast in comparison.' And a few days later he wrote to Moore: 'There is another man gone, about whom the world was ill-naturedly, and ignorantly, and brutally mistaken. It will, perhaps, do him justice *now*, when he can be no better for it.' The sentiments persisted, for five months later, on Christmas Day 1822, he wrote to Murray: 'You are all mistaken about Shelley – you do not know – how mild – how tolerant – how good he was in Society – and as perfect a Gentleman as ever crossed a drawing room – when he liked – and where he liked.'

II

The Happy Vagabonds

Rimbaud & Verlaine

Paul-Marie Verlaine was born at Metz in March 1844, the son of Captain Verlaine of the Engineers and Elisa Dehée, who had had a series of miscarriages during the first twelve years of her marriage until she finally produced Paul. Not unnaturally she lavished especial devotion on this son and heir after all her disappointments. He grew up spoilt and self-pitying, luxuriating in being the apple of his mother's eye. He was tall and slim, and most people regarded him as extremely ugly. 'He was like an orang-utan,' remarked the mother of one of his friends. His looks were not improved by the fact that he began to grow bald in his early twenties. Nevertheless he must have had some special charm of manner which compensated for his ugliness, for he never lacked for friends or lovers. He was bisexual, a propensity which had already shown itself in his school and college days, and there is no doubt that all his life he was capable of passionate relationships with both young men and women.

He was a good, though not a brilliant pupil in his school days. He said in later years that he was held to be a dunce, but when he left his *lycée* his master gave him an excellent testimonial. He was extremely musical and developed a pleasant singing voice. But his chief passion, early aroused, was for literature, especially poetry. In 1851 the Verlaines left Metz for good and migrated to Paris. There, in 1860, Paul met his lifelong friend, two years younger than himself, Edmond Lepelletier, who shared his enthusiasm for literature. Their parents had become close friends, and when they visited one another's homes the two boys used to shut themselves up in their rooms and gorge themselves on books, exploring not only French but English, Greek and Spanish in translation. Their early admirations included Victor Hugo and Théodore de Banville; but above all Baudelaire's *Fleurs du Mal*, which Verlaine had discovered by chance at school.

By the time he was twenty-one he was writing poetry himself. He attached himself to the new Parnassian movement, in which the young poets who grouped round it had found a sympathetic publisher in the bookseller Alphonse Lemène, whose rôle in their careers was not unlike that of Harold Monro, forty years later in London, with his Poetry Bookshop. The first collection of *Le Parnasse Contemporain* was published by him in 1866; Verlaine was •among the contributors. In the same year Lemène agreed to publish Verlaine's first book of poetry, *Poèmes Saturniens*. It consisted largely of imitative juvenilia, but nevertheless contained one of Verlaine's best remembered and most anthologized poems, which revealed both his musicality and his gift for evoking mood, which were to remain dominant characteristics of his poetry throughout his life, 'Chanson d'Automne':

> Les sanglots longs
> Des violons
> De l'automne

> Blessent mon coeur
> D'une langueur
>   Monotone,
> Et je pleure . . .

Three years later, in 1869, he published his second collection of poems, *Fêtes Galantes*. The distance between this and *Poèmes Saturniens* was striking. In this second book he showed that he had matured with extraordinary rapidity, displaying an assured technical accomplishment, a voice of his own and a highly developed sensibility. The warm friendship of many of the *Parnassiens*, and the generous encouragement of Mallarmé (which continued throughout his career) had helped to create a new poet of an individuality which could not be ignored.

The quarrels of the various literary cliques in nineteenth-century France (such a characteristically French phenomenon) are neither particularly edifying nor ultimately of great significance, but the *Parnassiens* represented a revolt against rhetoric and loose technical structure. Mallarmé was at that time associated with them, but already, as he developed his own purity of style and imaginative resonance, he was moving towards later recognition as one of the forerunners of that half-dreamlike, subjective mood that came to be called Symbolism. To us today he is mainly remembered as the author of 'L'Après-midi d'un Faune', which inspired, as a ballet, the music of Debussy and the choreography of Nijinski.

At this time another side of Verlaine's nature began to show itself. His favourite drink was absinthe, and his drinking bouts became more and more frequent. And when he was thoroughly drunk – which was not a state difficult for him to reach as absinthe was at that time extremely cheap – a more sinister element in his make-up was apt to emerge: he became violent, often uncontrollably, and would do things he bitterly repented when he was sober again.

In the same year, 1869, he met a girl of sixteen, Mathilde Mauté, who was graceful, of what seemed to Verlaine a sweet and innocent disposition, and, as she later showed only too clearly, a snob. The young poet fell at once, and decided that Mathilde, who knew nothing of his double nature as brilliantly gifted charmer and dangerous drunkard, as well as lover of both sexes, must be his future wife. Though Mathilde's father advised caution and delay, Mathilde and Verlaine began to correspond, and her suitor sent her poems (afterwards included in *La Bonne Chanson*) which enraptured her. Mathilde fell deeply in love, and by the winter they were engaged and family negotiations about dowries and settlements had begun. His intimate friend of lycée days, Lucien Viotti, refused at first to believe it, saying that Verlaine was totally unsuited to marriage. But Verlaine remained on his best behaviour, gentle, attentive and affectionate, and though he was reluctant Mathilde's father was finally persuaded to allow the marriage to take place earlier than after the two years he had at first stipulated. It was solemnized on 11 August 1870, only a few weeks after the Franco-Prussian War was declared. *La Bonne Chanson*, which Verlaine looked on as his wedding present to his wife, had been published in June.

During the hostilities, the siege of Paris by the Prussians, and the *Communard* regime which followed, Verlaine managed, by trickery and by luck, to keep his head down, though he scarcely emerged as a man of courage or principle. When order was restored, however, he found that he had

been dismissed from the post he had held in the Adminis-
tration of the *hôtel de ville*. Verlaine now had no salaried
post, and never had any official post again. The newly wed
couple moved into the Mautés' house in the rue Nicolet.

At that moment a letter arrived which was to change his
life. It was from a young man in Charleville, who signed
himself Arthur Rimbaud. He enclosed a batch of poems he
had recently written. Verlaine was impressed, and showed
them to several poet friends, who appear to have been
equally impressed. He then wrote the unknown poet a
famous letter inviting him to Paris: '*Venez, chère grande
âme, on vous appelle, on vous attend.*' He sent him some
money for his railway ticket, with the suggestion that he
should stay with him and his wife while in Paris.

Jean-Nicholas Arthur Rimbaud was born in October 1854
in the small town of Charleville on the outskirts of the
Ardennes near the Belgian frontier. He was the youngest
son in a family of four children. His father was a soldier who
distinguished himself in the Algerian wars, but left his wife
when Arthur was six years old and disappeared from view
for ever. His mother came from sound peasant or farm-
holding stock; she was a hard unimaginative woman of strict
moral views who believed in rigid discipline for her children.
Arthur came to hate her, but the fact that in the many crises
of his life he nearly always returned home suggests that
under her stern exterior a mother's natural feelings for her
children existed, a small fire but never entirely extinguished.

Arthur showed an astonishing intellectual precocity at
school, carrying off all the prizes. He made two especial
friends among his school-fellows, Ernest Delahaye and

Labarrière, but most important of all was the relationship that developed when he was fifteen between him and a master who had just arrived at the school, George Izambard, an unconventional man to find in the teaching profession, who loved literature, wrote himself, and had an ample library. A special sympathy of deep affection on both sides rapidly established itself between the master and his star pupil. Arthur hero-worshipped him, and his happiest hours were when he and Izambard were together, talking and reading. Izambard – who was only six years older than Rimbaud – allowed him the run of his library, and in addition not only enlarged and cultivated his literary taste but encouraged him in the poetry which he was beginning to write. It was astonishingly mature. In fact, the most astonishing thing about Rimbaud, what is almost impossible to believe, is that he wrote the poetry which has given him an unique place in French literature, including the prose poems of *Les Illuminations*, between the ages of fifteen and nineteen, when most young poets are fumbling with their final juvenilia, and then fell silent – for ever.

He longed more and more to get away from the provincial stuffiness of Charleville and his mother's repressive influence, and to discover the exciting literary world of Paris. He made his first, pathetic attempt to escape at the end of August 1870, boarded the train for Paris without a sou in his pockets, and was arrested on arrival for having travelled without a ticket. He was locked in prison, and was terrified. He wrote desperately to Izambard, begging him to come and rescue him. 'Do everything you can,' he wrote, 'I love you as a brother, and I'll love you as a father.' Izambard could not, however, go to Paris, but sent money to enable the boy to come to his home at Douai, as the advancing

Prussian armies made it impossible to go direct to Charleville. He stayed in Douai for three weeks, with Izambard's 'aunts', while his frantic mother tried to arrange to get him home. Eventually Izambard decided that there was nothing for it but to take him to Charleville himself.

It was little more than a month later that Rimbaud ran away again. He was found to have tramped all the way to Brussels, where he stayed with a friend of Izambard's, and then vanished. When Izambard, in a state of the greatest anxiety, returned from his searches to Douai, he found to his astonishment that Rimbaud had already established himself there and was busy copying out the poems he had written on his long walk. Some of these poems were among the happiest and least coarse he ever wrote, including the famous 'Ma Bohème', and 'Le Dormeur du Val' which was inspired by a soldier he found lying apparently asleep in a field but who was in fact dead with a hole in his forehead. At this period in his life, as 'Ma Bohème' shows, he was never happier than when tramping the countryside or city streets scribbling down the poems that came bubbling into his mind.

His mother now insisted, as he was a minor, that he should leave Douai at once and be brought back to her by the police. Before he left, Izambard made him promise not to run away again. Once back in Charleville he wrote to Izambard that he was suffocating in the atmosphere of his mother's home, but he would keep his promise to him, awful though the prospect was. 'The gratitude I feel for you, I can no more express it today than I could the other day. But I'm going to prove it to you. If it were only a question of doing something for you, I would die to do it. I give you my word of honour. I have a lot of things to say.'

In the end he did not keep his promise. The political

situation had changed radically. Napoleon III had surrendered to the Prussians at Sedan, but the Parisians refused to accept defeat and the *Gouvernement de la Défense Nationale* took over. Rimbaud spent his time with his friend Delahaye rambling round the countryside or finding a place where they could sit and smoke while Rimbaud read poetry aloud to Delahaye. He had discovered a new poet to put beside his idol Baudelaire: Paul Verlaine. Meanwhile the humiliating peace treaty was on the point of being signed. The radical National Guard grew in power and influence in Paris, and Rimbaud's sympathies were with them. The schools in Charleville and Mezières were reopened, but Rimbaud refused to return with Delahaye and Labarrière. Instead, he decided to slip back to Paris once more, and see how he could help the revolutionary forces that were gaining the upper hand. It was a disastrous impulse, and only brought him frustration and misery. He was, after all, only seventeen.

Paris was starving. Demoralized soldiers from the defeated armies came straggling in all the time. Everyone who had sufficient means had left, and in their place a rabble of thieves and hooligans poured in from the suburbs and further afield, intent on exploiting the city's misery. Rimbaud sold his watch to buy his ticket, and once in Paris went straight to the studio of the artist André Ghill, who was amazed to find the boy sleeping there when he came in. He gave him ten francs and told him to go straight back home, as there was nothing for a young poet in Paris. Rimbaud, however, did not go back to Charleville, but wandered about the streets in a state of total destitution, sleeping on park benches and under bridges and eating whatever scraps he could find in dumps and rubbish bins.

He met no one who could help him or put him in touch with any political group of any importance. Then something happened which made a deep and horribly painful mark on him. It seems that he approached the barracks in the rue de Babylone in order to sleep there, was subjected to unspecified indignities by the soldiers and possibly sexually assaulted. We shall probably never know what exactly happened, in spite of the assumption by many writers that the soldiers made the young girlish-looking boy their sexual plaything. In any case it was a searing experience of human degradation in which sexual activities certainly played their part. Out of it came the tragic poem 'Coeur Supplicié' (which was afterwards called 'Coeur Volé') which, full of misery and disgust as it is, is certainly capable of several interpretations, none of them pleasant:

> Mon triste coeur bave à la poupe,
> Mon coeur est plein de caporal:
> Ils y lancent des jets de soupe,
> Mon triste coeur bave à la poupe;
> Sous les quolibets de la troupe
> Qui pousse un rire général,
> Mon triste coeur bave à la poupe,
> Mon coeur est plein de caporal.

> Ithyphalliques et pioupiesques
> Leurs insultes l'ont dépravés !
> A la vesprée ils font des fresques
> Ithyphalliques et pioupiesques.
> O flots abracadabrantesques,
> Prenez mon coeur qu'il soit sauvé:
> Ithyphalliques et pioupiesques

The Happy Vagabonds

Leurs insultes l'ont dépravés! . . .*

The most tragic thing about the poem is that he sent it to his adored friend and master Izambard, with a note 'This is not a trifle!' But Izambard, from whom if from anyone he thought he could expect sympathy, failed entirely to take it seriously, and sent him a comic parody. The shock was overwhelming, and from that moment his trusting friendship with Izambard came to an end.

It was probably this experience in the rue de Babylone that made him suddenly decide to go home to Charleville at the beginning of March, just when the *Commune* was about to take over and his revolutionary hopes were about to be realized. He might have found some useful rôle in spite of his youth, though it is probably lucky that he did not. If the interpretation that 'Coeur Supplicié' refers to some brutal initiation into sex for a boy of sixteen who was still innocent and ignorant of the forms that sexual desire at its grossest could take, that would explain the precipitate flight from the scene of his degradation.

Rimbaud returned home a changed person. He refused to go back to school, took pleasure in looking as unkempt and disreputable as possible, and loitered round the cafés until he could find a friend to cadge a drink from. This was not generally too difficult, as in his cups he was good company, always ready to scandalize the more innocent with wildly indecent and blasphemous jokes and lewd stories of his exploits in Paris, which were probably more than half fantasy.

At the same time, beneath his mask of the disillusioned

* See Appendix I

78

young roué, concealing the true and so deeply shocking disillusionment, he was writing poems – remarkably original poems – to express his bitter contempt for all established conventions and beliefs, the scenes of crushed hopes and failures that he saw around him; though in many there sounded a note of sensitive pity for the victims that is truly Rimbaudian. And, at some period between March and September, he had begun work on what is his undoubted masterpiece, the long poem *Bateau Ivre*.

Meanwhile he showed his essential intellectual serious-ness in reading everything he could find in the public library that would feed the ideas that were gradually taking shape in his mind. He borrowed books from his friends, too, from one in particular with whom he had developed an especial friendship, Charles Bretagne. A customs officer by pro-fession, Bretagne was an altogether unusual character to find in a small provincial town. He was a skilled draughtsman and a fiddler, witty, genial and contemptuous of conven-tional bourgeois ideas. The new Rimbaud found him a sympathetic and congenial companion. More important for Rimbaud's development at this period, he was interested in magic and the occult, in alchemy and the esoteric doctrines of the Cabala. He lent Rimbaud books on these subjects, and talked to him endlessly about them. At the same time Rimbaud was reading deeply in Baudelaire, in whose works he found many of the same ideas, as it were in an undertone, in spite of the fact that Baudelaire never lost his Catholicism while Rimbaud was already basically an agnostic. Gradually these new ideas, with their heady intellectual and imagin-ative stimulus, began to dominate his thinking, and, almost unbelievably precocious as he was, led him to formulate his first aesthetic theories: what he believed a modern poet, breaking through all the rules and traditional poetic limits of the past – in particular the ideals of sterile technical perfection and impersonality that informed the work of the *Parnassiens* – should set as his goal. It was a formula for the total reconstruction of the personality of the poet, far more than merely his technique or inspirational moods, that he aimed to present in his famous 'Lettre du Voyant' which he wrote in May 1871. In fact there were two letters: the first to Izambard, the disastrous letter in which he had enclosed 'Le Coeur Supplicié'; the second a few days later, which he sent to Paul Démeny, Izambard's friend, a far longer and more explicit statement of his new revolutionary doctrines. Rather disjointed and interrupted as it is by poems that have no precise relevance, it reads more like notes for an eventual essay, but the main points he makes are absolutely clear, and one feels at times that they are like the utterances of someone in an hypnotic trance:

Here is some prose on the future of poetry.

All ancient poetry reaches its climax in Greek poetry. The harmonious life. From Greece to the romantic movement – middle ages – there are men of letters, versifiers. From Ennius to Theroldus, from Theroldus to Casimir Delavigne, everything is rhymed prose, a game, sloppiness and the glory of innumerable generations of idiots. Racine is the one pure one, the strong one, the great one . . . After Racine, the game grows mouldy. It has lasted two thousand years! . . .

No one has judged romanticism properly. Who would have judged it? The critics!! The romantics? Who proved so well that song is so rarely the real work, I mean thought in song and understood by the singer.

Because 'I' is someone else. If brass turns into a bugle, it's not in the least its fault. That's obvious to me: I help the development of my thought: I look at it, I listen to it: I aim an arrow at it: the symphony stirs in its depths, or comes in one bound to the surface.

If all those old imbeciles hadn't found the false significance of Me, we wouldn't have had to sweep away those millions of skeletons who, for longer than one can count, have piled up the products of their half-blind intelligence, claiming that they were writers! . . .

The first study of a man who wants to be a poet, is himself, the whole of himself; he looks for his soul, he examines it, he tests it, he gets to know it. Once he knows it, he must cultivate it! That seems simple. In everyone's mind a natural development takes place. So many *egoists* claim that they are authors: there are plenty of others who attribute their intellectual progress to themselves! But the point is that one must make one's soul monstrous: like the *comprachicos*, eh? Imagine a man making his face a mass of warts and cultivating them there.

I say that one must make oneself a *seer*, that one must become a *visionary*.

The poet makes himself a *seer* by a long, immense and deliberate *disordering of all his senses*. All forms of love, of suffering, of madness; he searches for his true self, he exhausts in himself all poisons, in order to keep only the quintessences. Unspeakable torture in which he needs all his faith, all his superhuman strength, in which he becomes among others the supreme sick man, the great criminal, the completely accursed one – and the supreme *savant*! – Because he reaches the *unknown*! Because he has cultivated his soul, already so rich, more than anyone else. He reaches the unknown, and when, in a state of craziness, he ends by losing the understanding of his visions, at least he has seen them. Let him die in his achievement of what is unheard of and unspeakable: other workers in the horrible will come after him; they will start in light of the horizons where the other one has reached his end . . .

So the poet is truly a stealer of fire.

He has taken charge of humanity, even the *animals*; he must make his inventions feel, throb, listen; if what he brings back from *the beyond* has form, he gives it form; if it has shapelessness, he lets it stay shapeless. To find a language; – in any case, as all speech is idea, the time for a universal language will come. One has to be an academic – more dead than a fossil – to spend one's efforts on a dictionary, in whatever language it may be . . . That language will be a soul for the soul, bringing together everything, perfumes, sounds, colours . . . The poet will define the amount of the unknown awakening in his time from the universal mind . . .

Such poets will come to pass! When the infinite servitude of woman shall at last have been broken, when she lives for herself and by herself, man – up to now abominable – having given her her liberty, she will be a poet, she too! She will discover the unknown. Will their ideas be different from ours? She will find things that are strange, unfathomable, shocking, delicious; we shall take them from them, we shall understand them!

Meanwhile we must ask a *poet* to give us something *new* – ideas and forms. All the clever ones would soon believe they had satisfied that need: – that's not it at all!

The first romantics were visionaries without properly

realizing it: the culture of their souls began with accidents: locomotives abandoned but burning, that remain on the rails for a time – Lamartine is sometimes a visionary, but strangled by ancient forms. The second wave of romantics are very much visionaries: Théophile Gautier, Leconte de Lisle, Théodore de Banville. But to catch a glimpse of the invisible and to hear the inaudible is something different from reproducing the spirit of what is dead, and Baudelaire is the first visionary, king of poets, a *real God*. At the same time he lived in too artistic a milieu, and his form which is so admired is petty. To invent the unknown one must have new forms . . .

And so my aim is to become a visionary.

Ever since he had begun his astonishingly precocious poetic career, there had grown in Rimbaud a belief, developed by his reading of occult books, but one cannot doubt primarily emerging from his own consciousness and reflection on his own immensely wide-ranging study of poetry and his own searing experiences, that behind the world appearances, of what our senses report to us, there is another world, a deeper truth and apprehension of our existence. As this belief grew, his desire to become a *voyant* through poetry and so to reach the unknown, whatever it might cost in happiness, dominated his mind and soul. If the 'Lettre du Voyant' is his first attempt to explain, *Bateau Ivre* is the first fruit in poetry of his new, exalted state of mind; though his other unique and enigmatic masterpiece, the sonnet 'Voyelles', probably written a little earlier, certainly hints at it. It is not known whether 'Voyelles' was one of the poems he brought with him to Paris when he accepted Verlaine's invitation, but *Bateau Ivre* (which Delahaye says he read to him on the eve of his departure) undoubtedly was, and must have convinced Verlaine that he had a genius on his hands in the seventeen-year-old poet who suddenly burst into his life.

What can one say of *Bateau Ivre* that has not been said before? It has been subject to innumerable interpretations of every kind, but it remains as mysterious, as unique and as profoundly inspiring to anyone of fresh poetic sensibility as on the day it was written. Rimbaud had never seen the sea when he wrote it, but it is an account of a dream voyage as intensely vivid as if the author had passed a lifetime on ships at sea and had been granted visions of the ocean, its terrors and wonders, that no one voyager could ever have experienced. The substratum contains all the stories of the sea that had so enthralled him as a boy, but transformed by Rimbaud's imagination into a spiritual experience through imagery of the utmost originality and evocative power. The richness of the language, the mastery of rhythmic structure are almost incredible for a boy of seventeen. Nobody can read it without being haunted by it, especially again and again by certain dazzling lines, such as:

> Je sais le soir,
> L'aube exaltée ainsi qu'un peuple de colombes,
> Et j'ai vu quelquefois ce que l'homme a cru voir!

Or such images as:

> Plus douce qu'aux enfants la chair des pommes sures
> L'eau verte penetra ma coque de sapin . . .

and most hauntingly and mysteriously:

Est-ce en ces nuits sans fonds que tu dors et t'exiles,
Millions d'oiseaux d'or, O future vigueur?

In some ways most strange and most poignant of all is the
apparent renunciation of his visions, as if they were too
terrible, too great a burden to bear, in the last stanzas in
which he recalls the child 'plein de tristesse', who had once
been happy to launch, on a village puddle: 'Un bateau frêle
comme un papillon de mai'.

Verlaine and his friend Charles Cros went to the station to
meet Rimbaud, but by the time they got there the train had
come in and there was no sign of him. He had gone straight
to the Mauté home in the rue Nicolet where Verlaine and his
wife had installed themselves. When Verlaine arrived he was
astonished to see before him not the young man of twenty or
twenty-one Rimbaud's letters had led him to suppose, but a
gawky boy with pink cheeks, a mop of tousled reddish
brown hair, huge hands that stuck out from a coat that was
too small for him, and unforgettably piercing blue eyes. He
was dirty from his journey, and shy and nervous, which
made him surly with the two rather bewildered women.

The evening was a total disaster. Mathilde and her mother
attempted during dinner to keep up polite social chatter, and
the men to draw their guest out with discussion of literary
matters. Rimbaud's answers were monosyllabic if he
answered at all, and at the end of the meal he drew out his
pipe and began to smoke his coarse tobacco. Everyone
appeared dismayed if not horrified, though one cannot help
feeling that Verlaine must have seen the funny side of it,
especially when Madame Mauté's pampered little dog

appealed to Rimbaud for some scraps, and Rimbaud made one of his few remarks of the evening: '*Les chiens, ce sont des libéraux!*'

The visit continued on its disastrous course. Mathilde, who was eight months pregnant, became more and more disgusted with their guest and her husband's indulgent attitude towards him. The respectable life was only the thinnest veneer over Verlaine's natural propensities; and there is no doubt that with Rimbaud he began to drink heavily again. Monsieur Mauté de Fleurville, who had been on a shooting expedition in the country, returned home and immediately demanded that Rimbaud should be sent packing. He did not wait to be turned out, but walked out, and it appears that it was only some days – or perhaps weeks – later that Verlaine found him wandering the streets. He managed to find him lodging with various of his friends for brief periods, including the kind and indulgent Théodore de Banville. Eventually, when his friends' patience was exhausted, he rented a room for him off the Boulevard Montparnasse, in the rue Campagne-Première.

It is not known exactly when Verlaine and Rimbaud became lovers, but there seems little doubt that it was about this time. There can also be no doubt at all that they did become lovers, not only in the judgement of many of their friends, but also in the light of one of the poems Verlaine wrote some years later, 'Laeti et Errabundi' (Happy Vagabonds), and the even more explicit poem, his unashamed celebration of homosexual love in comparison with the conventional discoveries of 'normal' love, beginning 'Ces passions qu'eux seuls nomment encore amours'. Before this Verlaine had developed passionate relationships with adolescents of his own sex, and Rimbaud, determined as he was to break all conventional bourgeois rules (though it appears with little earlier experience), was a willing pupil who soon became the dominant partner in the relationship. One must accept that this sexual side to their association was not simply an audacious experiment, but one that gave them both happiness and fulfilment, as the two poems I have just mentioned make perfectly clear.

Scandal was not slow in raising its head. Verlaine ceased to bother about his appearance, preferring to look as disreputable as Rimbaud did. One evening they went together to the first night of a play at the Théâtre-Français in their most dishevelled clothes, and a malicious journalist reported next morning that among the men of letters who were present 'was noticed Paul Verlaine, the poet, giving his arm to a charming young lady, Mlle. Rimbaud'. Verlaine's doting mother called at the rue Nicolet, found that her son had been absent for some days, and was horrified to learn that in the previous six weeks he had run through 2,000 francs. Obviously he had spent most of it on Rimbaud and on their drinking-bouts together. One of Verlaine's excuses for staying away from home was that he was sitting for Fantin–Latour's 'Le Coin de Table', which was to portray a group of up and coming young writers of the time. Verlaine appears sitting on the far left-hand side, with an angelic-looking Rimbaud beside him. This is the only painting of Rimbaud that exists, though there are many drawings and caricatures of him mostly made by Verlaine himself, and one photograph taken by Carjat at about this time, in which Rimbaud looks very much less angelic. On the right-hand side of Fantin-Latour's famous picture is a pot of geraniums, put there to take the place allotted to Albert Mérat, who had refused to appear in such a collection of 'pimps and thieves', obviously meaning Verlaine and Rimbaud, as the rest of the group look highly respectable.

Meanwhile things were going from bad to worse in the rue Nicolet. Mathilde became all too painfully aware of the other side of the man she had married. On 30 October 1871 their son Georges was born. For three days Verlaine behaved like a model father, affectionate and solicitous. Then the absences began again, Verlaine suddenly reappearing, totally drunk and making terrible scenes. One evening, when the baby was about three months old, he arrived home in one of his violent drunken moods, seized the baby and flung it against the wall. Luckily no serious injury was done. Mathilde, having confessed to her parents what had been going on, left with the baby, its nurse and her father for six weeks in the country.

There is little doubt that Verlaine spent most of these six weeks with Rimbaud, drinking with him in the cafés, talking endlessly about poetry, and making love with him in the rue Campagne-Première. A number of critics and biographers, including Enid Starkie and Joanna Richardson, have concerned themselves quite seriously with the question whether the two lovers practised sodomy with one another. But as in any case there are many other ways – as the poem 'Ces Passions' frankly describes – in which two males can make love to one another, this seems of comparatively trifling significance. It seems possible that Rimbaud was basically more heterosexual than homosexual, and that it was Verlaine who initiated him into their love-making. But once they became lovers it is likely that Rimbaud, as a far stronger character, was the leading spirit.

Mathilde knew nothing of this. She only knew that since they had been together Verlaine's behaviour had appallingly deteriorated, and her instinct told her that Rimbaud was depraving him. She answered his affectionate letters in a way that showed she still loved him. She was ready to come back to him, but she made one condition: Rimbaud must leave Paris. Verlaine stalled. Mathilde played her strongest card, and threatened to ask her solicitor to file a request for separation. Verlaine gave way, and Rimbaud left Paris.

When Mathilde returned, Verlaine was again on his best behaviour. It did not last: Rimbaud had slipped back into Paris. The violent scenes started again, and Mathilde became really frightened. One morning, when he seemed perfectly calm, he kissed his wife goodbye; then he left the rue Nicolet, never to return as her husband.

Some days later she received a letter from him in Brussels, then a second letter in which he told her he had come into contact with some *Communard* refugees there, and planned to write a history of the *Commune*. Would she send him his papers? She emptied his desk, claiming afterwards that none of the drawers was locked, and among the papers, which included letters from literary friends congratulating him on his last book of poems, *La Bonne Chanson*, she found some letters from Rimbaud. They were love letters, and though she did not fully understand them in her innocence at the time, they horrified her. 'I thought they had been written by a madman,' she wrote later. She burst into tears, and her father, hearing her, came into the room and seized the papers: a glance made him realize how useful they would be in any legal action against her husband. Among the papers he took was a long poem by Rimbaud which was in an envelope by itself. This was 'La Chasse Spirituelle', which Verlaine thought was his greatest poem. No trace of it has ever been found. Nevertheless, Mathilde decided to make one more effort to get him back. She left for Brussels with her mother. On the way she had an idea: she would propose that they leave for New Caledonia, where they had some ex–*Communard* friends. The baby would be left with the Mautés.

Verlaine agreed, apparently enthusiastically. They decided to go back to Paris together the next day and make preparations. Verlaine was there on the platform at the time arranged, but he had seen Rimbaud again and was drunk. At the frontier station all passengers had to get out for customs examination. Verlaine disappeared, though they searched everywhere. As the doors were being slammed, they suddenly caught sight of him. 'Hurry up!' cried Madame Mauté. But Verlaine shouted back: 'No, I'm staying.' Rimbaud, it seems more than likely, had been on the train and followed him into the station bar.

The two friends remained for two months in Belgium, then decided to cross over to England in September. There was a large number of French journalists, artists and intellectuals in Soho at the time, mostly exiled ex-*Communards*. They helped the newcomers to find a room off Tottenham Court Road, at 35 Howland Street.

Before they left for England, in fact only a few days after he abandoned her at the frontier, Verlaine wrote an abusive letter to Mathilde: 'Miserable carrot fairy (*fée carotte*), mean little mouse princess, filthy tick just waiting for two fingers to throw you into the pot! You've done me every injury you could; you have perhaps destroyed my friend's heart. I am going to join Rimbaud again, if he wants to have me after the treachery you've made me commit.'

Mathilde promptly gave the letter to her father, and asked

him to go ahead definitively with the proceedings for a legal separation. Verlaine continued to write to her, but she put his letters away unopened; he had become a horror to her. Five years later, she tells us, she brought herself to open them, and realized that, in some twisted and fuddled part of his mind, he had come to see himself as the wronged one, a misunderstood martyr who only asked to be allowed to forgive her – though much more rarely he asked to be allowed to forgive himself. His capacity for self-deception and self-dramatization was boundless, as always before and after.

We have glimpses of the first impressions of London from Verlaine's letters to Edmond Lepelletier. They were unhappy at first, depressed by the soot-blackened houses, the general atmosphere of squalor and the gruesomeness of the English Sunday with its restrictions on drinking and every sort of enjoyment, and the fish in the restaurants that was cooked till it looked like octopus. Gradually, however, they found aspects that amused and fascinated them: the young boot-blacks in their scarlet coats who polished anyone's boots for a penny a time from early morning till night, the barrel-organs, the music-halls with their boisterous songs and good humour. In October Verlaine wrote: 'The fog is beginning to show the filthy tip of its nose. Everyone is coughing here except me. It's true – you know me – that I'm swaddled in flannel mufflers, cotton-wool in the ears, and other precautions which are as sensible here as they are silly in Paris.' They were delighted with the British Museum, where they could study any book they wanted. Above all they were entranced with the London docks: 'The docks are unheard-of: Carthage, Tyre and everything in one.' No doubt dock-land made an even deeper impression on Rimbaud, with his unassuaged dreams of vast oceans and exotic islands and continents beyond them.

In Howland Street both poets appear to have worked hard: Verlaine at his *Romances sans Paroles*, the book which showed Rimbaud's influence most clearly and which was originally to have been dedicated to him; and Rimbaud most probably at his earliest pieces in the *Illuminations*. There was much less opportunity for dissipation in London, and as the 'Paysages Belges' in *Romances sans Paroles* clearly indicates, Verlaine's poetic impulse was more than ever awake; and awake in a new way, unmistakably influenced by Rimbaud's ideas and manner. The 'Ariettes Oubliées', with which the volume opens, and the 'Paysages Belges' are the most Rimbaudian poems Verlaine ever wrote, and to some of his admirers his finest, in their uninhibited innovations in language and style, their affinity with popular songs and rhythms, and so often far less overtly expressive of deeply personal moods than had been his wont. As far as he could, he seemed to be following the principle that Rimbaud had announced in the 'Lettre du Voyant' as the goal of the new poetry he dreamed of, the anti-sentimental visionary poetry of the future, '*Je est un autre.*' Nevertheless I think one has to read between the lines to discover glimpses of the depth of the relationship that now bound them so closely, intellectually, emotionally and physically.

The commentators and scholars have always been in dispute as to when Rimbaud wrote *Les Illuminations*; some maintaining that he wrote them all in London, before Verlaine's imprisonment and before he retired to the family farm at Roche to write *Une Saison en Enfer*; others that some were added after that traumatic event. What is at least certain is that he was at work on the earliest of them when (or even before) he was in England with Verlaine. Rimbaud never put them into any coherent order himself, and when they reached *La Vogue*, the Symbolist review edited by Gustave Kahn, either from Verlaine himself or from his brother-in-law Charles de Sivry, Rimbaud himself was far away in Abyssinia and knew nothing of their publication in *La Vogue* or their subsequent publication as a volume. In his introduction to this volume, Verlaine said that the title, *Illuminations*, was taken from the English, meaning coloured illustrations or plates. It is equally clear, however, that the title was meant also to have the meaning of 'moments of vision or hallucinations'. No one can read them without feeling that in these '*poèmes non versifiés*' Rimbaud reached the furthest point in his search which he had announced as his aim in the *Lettre du Voyant*, to find a new way of describing both the world of experience and the world of the visionary, the way through the 'disordering of all the senses' (*dérèglement de tous les sens*). It is possible that some of them are transcriptions of hallucinations experienced under the influence of drugs, but what is important is the poetic form Rimbaud gave these hallucinations; and what is particularly fascinating is the way in which he returns again and again to the impressions, untouched by later experience or reading, of childhood. In a remarkable essay on Rimbaud, the Greek poet Demetrios Capetanakis writes discerningly of the inherent contradictions in these works of genius:

The *Illuminations* are an attempt to blow up all appearances, all orders, all forms of the world, which make our happiness. They are an attempt to blow up all happiness and make a work of pure unhappiness out of the debris and fragments of the explosion. But how strange! These fragments are not pieces of dirt and ugliness. They are not disgusting like pieces of a blown-up body. They have a strange, fascinating beauty. They are like precious stones and broken tender whispers . . . This heap of fragments from all possible orders, which should reveal to us what lies beyond all orders of the world, beyond all happiness, rises before us like a glorious rainbow speaking to us of the sweetness of pleasure . . . How they shine, how they sparkle before us, all these diamonds and this foam, these drops of sweat and these eyes, these rays and their floating hair, these flames and this herbage of steel and emerald, these white, burning tears and these ringing, flashing dream flowers, these swarms of gold leaves, these balls of sapphire and these angels of the *Illuminations*! Real fireworks to make us happy. And to think that they were meant to fight our happiness, to make us wake up and grow out of it! Happiness is always the winner. Even the works created to destroy happiness become one more happiness in the world.

Verlaine believed that Rimbaud's greatest achievement in these poems was in language – in style. He wrote with enthusiastic admiration of their '*prose exquise*' and '*la plus haute ambition (arrivée) du style*'. Poems such as these, in whatever order one places them and whatever interpretation one discovers in them (and many of them are so arcane as almost to defy the labour or inspiration of interpretation) achieve their intention of being poetry and not prose in another form, by their use of language and imagery of the most startling innovation, by their original way of looking at the world that has none of the forced bravura of the surrealists and, abandoning traditional forms, by their use of internal rhymes, assonance and a logic of structure that is of poetry and not of prose – and the work of a master craftsman as well as visionary.

Before he embarked on the *Illuminations* and the miraculous songlike poems which he inserted in the *Saison en Enfer*, Rimbaud wrote a number of poems in verse – apart from 'La Chasse Spirituelle', which has so disastrously disappeared. Unless one counts the songlike masterpieces, they were his last in traditional forms: mainly of four-line alexandrine stanzas, though their technical originality takes them far from the Parnassian and other much vaunted high-lights of contemporary traditional poetry. It is possible that not all have survived, but 'Mémoire', 'La Rivière de Cassis' and 'Michel et Christine' testify to his increasing virtuosity and originality, and also, one cannot help feeling, to his sense at this time of loneliness, of being marked out for a poetic destiny no others could share. The song-poems, interspersed so mysteriously in the *Saison en Enfer*, are in my opinion the climax of his poetry as he wanted it to be, perfect in their concentrated yet simple-seeming expressiveness, haunting as nothing else written at that time and giving a strange feeling of joy in the midst of the complex images and moods from which they are distilled. Once read, one returns to them again and again, with them ringing in one's mind never to be forgotten.

The two poets stayed together in Howland Street, writing furiously and exploring London, until Christmas, when Rimbaud left for Charleville. This was quite possibly on the advice of his mother, who showed him more maternal concern than she had appeared to be capable of before; at the same time she was beginning a sympathetic relationship with Verlaine's mother. They were both filled with anxiety about the accusations of immorality that were likely to be made in the legal proceedings for separation. Verlaine was left lamenting: 'The emptiness is dreadful! I don't care about anything else.' All the time, quite futilely and perversely, he was still dreaming of the possibility of a reconciliation with his wife. He summoned his mother to London and talked of renting a little house where they could live together – to give him *respectability*. After a month's absence Rimbaud, summoned by telegram, returned. They stayed together till the beginning of April, then crossed back to Belgium. Verlaine was still afraid that if he ventured on to French soil he might be arrested for his activities in the *Commune*, which were trifling enough.

They appear to have had a week together in Brussels, before Rimbaud decided to retire to Roche, and work at what were probably *Les Illuminations* and *Une Saison en Enfer*. Verlaine had taken rooms only a few miles away, and probably saw Rimbaud from time to time. Finally he persuaded him to attempt to live with him again in London: he could not live with him, he could not live without him. On this occasion they took a room in Camden Town, at what was then 8 Great College Street. Here Verlaine fully discovered the 'poetry of London' he had hoped to find on his first visit. 'London is delightful,' he wrote to his friend Blémont, 'this neighbourhood is very gay. In the north west the countryside is lovely.' He described his explorations there, his frequent visits to the wonderful British Museum Library, and the French lessons he was giving to English pupils, which just managed to keep him in funds – with the aid of remittances from his mother. But relations with

Rimbaud remained stormy. It seems that they quarrelled as much as they made love together. The younger poet was changing, and began to delight in tormenting him, and to be exasperated with his continual harping on a reconciliation with his wife. Verlaine threatened suicide, but soon abandoned the impulse. At the beginning of July he found himself at the end of his tether. He left the house, and embarked on a ship to take him back to Belgium. Rimbaud rushed to the quayside, overcome with anxiety and remorse, and signalled to Verlaine to leave the ship and come back to him. Verlaine paid no attention; yet on board ship he wrote to Rimbaud saying that their rows had become too much for him and it was clear that they couldn't live together. If he couldn't be reconciled with his wife, he would blow his brains out: 'If, which is very unlikely, I'm obliged to perform this last pitiable act, I shall, at least, do it bravely. My last thought will be of you, for you who were beckoning to me, this afternoon, from the quayside, when I wouldn't go back, because it's necessary that I should die. Nevertheless! I embrace you before I die.'

While Verlaine was writing his histrionic letter, Rimbaud was writing to him, a letter full of self-accusation and love: an extraordinary document, revealing the other side of their ambiguous relationship, more clearly than any other correspondence that has survived between them. It is dated Friday afternoon, 4 July:

Come back, come back, dearest friend, my only friend, come back. I swear to you that I shall be good to you. If I was ill-humoured with you, it was a joke I got into the habit of, and I am more sorry than I can say. Come back, it will all be forgotten. How disastrous that you should have taken it so seriously. I have been crying for the last two days. Come back. Be brave, dearest friend. Nothing is lost. You have only to make your journey back to me. We'll live here together again, we shall be brave and patient. Oh, I beg you. It is in your own interest too. Come back, and you'll find all your things here. I hope you know now there was nothing real in our quarrel. That horrible moment! But you – when I signalled to you to leave the ship, why didn't you come? We have lived together for two years, and then that happens! What are you going to do? If you don't want to come back here, do you want me to come and find you wherever you are?

Yes, I was in the wrong. – Oh, you won't forget me, will you? – No, you can't ever forget me. – I was always there for you. – Tell me, tell your friend, – must we never live together any more? – Be brave. Answer me quickly. – I can't stay here for much longer. – Only listen to what your heart tells you. – Hurry! Tell me if I am to rejoin you.

All my life is yours.

Rimbaud

Hurry I can't stay here later than Monday morning. If I can't see you again, I shall enlist in the navy or the army. Oh, come back, I begin crying again and again. Tell me to come to you and I'll come . . .

When Verlaine's letter reached him, Rimbaud's despairing frenzy had grown calmer. Nevertheless, he wrote back a letter still full of love, though with a rather more ominous tone:

[London 5 July 1873]

I have your letter dated 'at sea' . . .

Only with me can you be free, and since I swear that I'll be nice to you in future, that I am deeply sorry for my part in what went wrong, that I have at last a perfectly clear feeling, that I love you very much, if you don't want to come back, or want to join me again, you will be committing a crime and will repent it for many years, owing to your loss of all liberty and suffer distress more terrible than what you have already suffered. After that, think again about what you were before you got to know me.

As for me, I am not going back to my mother. I am going to Paris. I shall try and leave on Monday evening. You will have obliged me to sell all your clothes. I can't do otherwise. They aren't already sold: they'll only take them away on Monday morning. If you want to send letters to me in Paris, send them care of L. Forain, 289 rue St Jacques (for A. Rimbaud). He'll know my address.

Quite certainly if your wife comes back to you, I shall not compromise you by writing to you. I shan't ever write.

The only thing that means anything is: come back. I want to be with you. I love you. If you listen to that you will show courage and a spirit of sincerity.

Otherwise, I blame you.

But I love you, I embrace you and we shall see one another again.

After this exchange of letters, Verlaine became more frantic than before. He wrote to his mother announcing that he was going to commit suicide. She hurried to Brussels to dissuade him. At the same time he wrote to Mathilde, telling her that if she didn't return to him within a certain number of days he would kill himself. Knowing Verlaine she ignored the letter. Verlaine, as anyone who understood him might have predicted, abandoned the idea of suicide, and sent a telegram to Rimbaud begging him to join him in Brussels. Rimbaud arrived on 8 July, and was soon driven to exasperation by Verlaine's hysterical mixture of threats and imploring appeals. He found himself unable to tolerate his state of hysteria, and told him he was determined to go back to Paris, whether Verlaine came with him or not. Verlaine rushed out to buy a revolver and get drunk, and when he and Rimbaud met again fired at him three times. He wounded Rimbaud in the wrist, but the other two shots went astray. He rushed to his mother in the next room, and abandoned himself to despair. His mother persuaded him to take the wounded Rimbaud to hospital with her. The wound was not serious, but Rimbaud announced that he intended to go back at once to his mother at Charleville. On the way to the station Verlaine, still in a drunken state of incoherent frenzy, turned to Rimbaud and made as if to shoot him again. Rimbaud rushed for protection to an *agent de police*, who arrested Verlaine: at the police station he was charged with attempted murder. About a week later the bullet was extracted from Rimbaud's wrist, and as soon as he was on his feet again he went to the law courts where he made a statement asserting that the shooting was an accident. The charge against Verlaine was reduced to one of criminal assault. At the trial, the doctors who had examined him in prison claimed that they had found proof of active and passive sodomy. The claim would be treated as totally unreliable and absurd in a modern court of law, but it obviously influenced the court powerfully against Verlaine. The judge sentenced him to two years' hard labour, and a fine of 200 francs.

In view of the scandal that had been created and had become the talk of Paris, it would clearly have been unwise, even if it had been possible, for the two friends to communicate with one another while Verlaine was in prison. Rimbaud retired to his mother's farm at Roche, and in spite of the fact that it was harvest time shut himself up in his room to complete *Une Saison en Enfer*. He was frequently to be heard sobbing bitterly, according to those of his family who passed his room. Everything was in ruins for him, his friendship with Verlaine – perhaps the only great passion he ever experienced – and the dreams out of which he had convinced himself that he was a *voyant*, almost a god who could not only create a new poetry but transform the beliefs of human beings in his age.

In his remarkable essay on Rimbaud, which I have already quoted, Demetrios Capetanakis wrote:

To go out of the world was Rimbaud's great desire ever since he discovered how deceptive life in the world can be . . . He thought, since the world is only a world of appearances and since behind all these appearances we always find the same dark and inconceivable something, the unknown, this unknown must be the reality in which we should live if we wanted to have a real and undeceived life. And determined to conquer this real and undeceived life he set to work, we already know how. By deranging everything – as much as he could and as many as possible of the orders of the world. He made himself homeless, an expatriate, an outlaw in love and in poetry, the sworn enemy of reason and happiness, he did everything he could not to belong to the world, to abstract himself from it, always on the look-out for an opportunity to go completely out of it. Not by suicide. He did not want to go out of the world as nothing into nothing, but as a traveller going to an unknown country to explore it, to know it and to live in it. Poetry and friendship were the two most important ways he tried for this exit from the world. He went both these ways to their limits, beyond which there is neither poetry nor friendship, but eternal silence and separation . . .

In August 1873 Rimbaud finished his work on *Une Saison en Enfer*, which he had originally called *Livre Païen ou Livre Nègre*, to indicate that it had nothing to do with his Catholic upbringing or Christianity, though it is difficult to accept that as a final interpretation.

Many critics and commentators have taken the view that Rimbaud wished his *Saison en Enfer* to be his total farewell to poetry and that he was indifferent to its fate. But the history of the work, as we now know it, cannot sustain that view. He was determined to have the work printed, by himself (with his mother's aid), and, after he had corrected the proofs with considerable care, sent copies of it to his friends in the literary world of Paris. 'My fate depends on this book,' he had told his friend Delahaye, which surely means that he still had hope of literary fame in his immediate lifetime. A story circulated at one time that when he found himself cold-shouldered (and how horribly) by the literary world when he visited Paris, he not only burnt all his papers, but also destroyed all the copies that remained of *Une Saison en Enfer*. This story is belied by the fact that eventually, many years later, a large number of copies was found in the printer's premises, quite simply because the bill had never been paid.

This is not a critical study of either of the two great poets with which it concerns itself, but as *Une Saison en Enfer* is essentially a spiritual biography of Rimbaud, and deals in its central sections with the relationship between Verlaine and Rimbaud, it is essential to examine it with some attention, especially as Rimbaud himself set such store by it.

Une Saison en Enfer is a work of explosive and brilliantly complex confessional rhetoric, written in all too evident and searing spiritual agony, in what Verlaine was to call '*prose de diamant*', where every word has its full force and no word is fudged or superfluous, coruscating with the imagery that had been so remarkable in the *Illuminations*; and though its argument and conclusion admit of more than one inter-pretation from the religious point of view – about which the critics have endlessly debated – it is basically the story of how Rimbaud came to believe he was almost a god himself, capable of creating a new heaven and earth through poetry, of discovering a deeper reality behind the appearance of everyday life and everyday attitudes, and how that dream, that hallucination perhaps one should call it, finally failed him. He had been born in a deeply Christian entourage, he had been baptized, he felt himself in a certain sense doomed to the Christian atmosphere, though one cannot believe that at the end he had reached total acceptance of what he had denied as a *voyant*. One has to remember that when he started to write this unique work of genius – the work of a young man who had hardly left his teens – he called it, as I have said, *Livre Païen ou Nègre*, that is the declaration of someone who felt himself or wanted to present himself as anterior to or untouched by the Christian tradition.

In 'Alchémie du Verbe' ('Délires II'), he writes:

> For a long time I boasted of knowing all possible land-scapes, and found the celebrated works of modern painting and poetry ridiculous.
>
> I liked idiotic pictures, paintings above doors, stage scenery, acrobats' back-cloths, sign-boards, popular prints in colours, old-fashioned literature, Church Latin, badly spelt erotic works, novels that appealed to our grandfathers, fairy tales, little children's books, old operas, silly rhymes, naif rhythms.
>
> I dreamed of crusades, voyages of discovery that have never been described, republics unknown to history, religious wars that were suppressed, revolutions in morals, migrations of races and continents: I believed in all enchanted stories.
>
> I invented the colours of vowels! A black, E white, I red, O blue, U green. I made rules for the shape and movement of all consonants, and with the aid of instinctive rhythms, I pleased myself with the idea that I had invented a kind of poetry that one day would have its meaning for all the senses. I kept my translation rights . . .

In his 'Farewell', in his most hallucinated manner, he writes:

> Sometimes I see in the sky endless beaches crowded with white nations, all rejoicing. A great golden ship waves the many colours of its sails above me in the morning breezes.

I have created every kind of festival, all triumphs, all dramas. I have tried to invent new flowers, new stars, new kinds of living flesh, new languages. I imagined I had acquired supernatural powers. Well, I must bury all these things I have imagined, and my memories! A splendid fame as an artist and teller of stories, all gone.

As for me, who called myself sorcerer or angel, exempt from all moral rules, I have now returned to the earth, with a duty to look for, and a rough reality to embrace. Peasant!

Une Saison en Enfer is divided into nine chapters, with a seasonal sequence, beginning with spring and ending with autumn. The central chapters, 'Délires I' ('La Vierge Folle', 'L'Epoux Infernal') and 'Délires II' ('Alchémie du Verbe'), are those devoted to his relationship with Verlaine, though it is possible to see in 'L'Epoux Infernal' a double rôle for the narrator, who may in part be Rimbaud himself as well as Verlaine. One must nevertheless assume that the confession of 'L'Epoux Infernal' is essentially an extraordinary empathetic act of Rimbaud putting himself dramatically into the mind of Verlaine during their relationship:

O divine Bridegroom, my Lord [he begins] refuse not to hear the confession of the most sorrowful of your hand-maidens. I am lost, I am drunken, I am unclean. What a life!

His mysteriously tender ways seduced me. I forgot all my obligations as a human being to follow him. What a life! it has nothing to do with real life. We are not in the world, I go where he goes. I have to. And often he flies into a rage against me – against me, wretched soul! The

Demon! He is a demon, you know, *he is not a man* . . .
When he seemed downcast, I would follow him in all his
strange and complicated actions, good or evil. I was
certain I would never enter his world. Beside his beloved
sleeping body, how many hours, how many nights I lay
awake, trying to understand why he wished so much to
escape from reality. Never did any man have such a
dedication. I realized – without feeling afraid for him –
that he was capable of becoming a grave danger to society.
Perhaps he has secrets for transforming life? No, I told
myself, he is only looking for them. In fact, his loving
kindness is a kind of sorcerer's spell, and I am its prisoner . . .

Then with a grief that was endlessly renewed, and with
a feeling of bewilderment in my own eyes – as in the eyes
of all who would willingly have turned to me, if I had not
been condemned for ever to be forgotten by all, – I
became hungrier than ever for his kindness. With his
kisses and tender embraces I was indeed in heaven, I
entered a dark heaven, where I would have wished to be
left, poor, deaf, dumb and blind. I was already becoming
used to it. I saw us as two good children, free to walk
together in a Paradise of sorrow. We were at one in this.
Deeply moved, we worked together. But after a
passionate embrace, he would say: 'How queer you will
find all this you have gone through with me, when I am no
longer with you. When you no longer have my arms
under your neck, nor my heart to rest on, nor this mouth
on your eyes. For I shall have to go away one day, yes far
away. For I shall have to go to the aid of others. Although
I shall not find much pleasure in it . . . dear soul . . .

Ah, I have never been jealous of him. I don't think he

will leave me. What would happen to him? He doesn't know anybody. He'll never work. Would his goodness and his kindness by themselves give him any help in the real world? He wants to live like a sleep-walker. At times I forget the pitiful state into which I have fallen. He will give me strength, we shall travel, we shall hunt in the deserts, we shall sleep on the pavements of unknown cities, with no troubles and no cares. Or I shall wake up, and find that laws and customs have changed – thanks to his magic power; or the world will remain the same, and will leave me to my desires, my joys, my calm moments of indifference . . .

One day perhaps he will disappear as if by magic. But I must be told of it, if he is to rise again to some heaven, so that I may see the assumption of my lover.

Rimbaud's ironic concluding comment on this whole imagined confession is quite simply: '*Drôle de ménage!*' ('What a queer couple!')

While Rimbaud was writing this at Roche, Verlaine wrote a poem in prison which is in a sense his own comment on the affair, on Rimbaud's dream of godlike power and his disillusionment. He calls the poem 'Crimen Amoris', the first version of which is the most forceful. He imagines a celebration of 'Satan's adolescents' of the seven mortal sins, dominated by one, the most beautiful, obviously intended for Rimbaud:

> Or, le plus beau d'entre tous ces mauvais anges
> Avait seize ans sous sa couronne de fleurs.
> Croissant ses bras sur les colliers et les franges,
> Il songeait l'oeil plein de flammes et de pleurs . . .

Then this 'adolescent of Satan' makes an impassioned speech, beginning 'Oh je serai celui-là qui créera Dieu'; and coming to a climax with these verses:

Vous le saviez, qu'il n'est point de différence
Entre ce que vous denommez Bien et Mal,
Qu'au fond des deux vous n'avez que la souffrance,
Je veux briser ce pacte trop anormal

Il ne faut plus de ce schisme abominable!
Il ne faut plus d'enfer et de paradis!
Il faut l'Amour ! Meure Dieu! Meure le Diable!
Il faut que le bonheur soit seul, je vous dis! . . .

La torche tombe de sa main éployée,
Et l'incendie alors hurla s'élevant,
Querelle énorme d'aigles rouges noyée
Au remous noir de la fumée et du vent,

Et les Satans mourants chantaient dans les flammes,
Ayant compris, ils étaient fiers et joyeux
Et ce beau choeur de voix d'hommes et de femmes
Flambait avec les pavillons somptueux. . .

Les bras tendus au ciel comme vers son frère,
Un grand sourire aux lèvres, il s'exaltait;
Quand retentit un affreux coup de tonnerre.
Tout s'éteignit. . .Seul un rossignol chantait.

On n'avait pas agréé le sacrifice
Quelqu'un de fort et de juste assurément,
Au nom du ciel provoqué, faisant l'office
De justicier, envoyait ce châtiment.

Du Haut Palais aux cent tours, pas un vestige,

Rien ne resta dans ce désastre inouï
Afin que par un formidable prestige
Ceci ne fût qu'un rêve évanoui. . .*

The poem ends with a prayer to the 'Dieu clément qui nous sauvera du mal', very much in the redeemed mood of 'La Vierge Folle'.

We do not know how long Rimbaud spent in Paris after his humiliating experience, nor who, among his previous friends, remained loyal to him. There is a blank in his life between November 1874 and February 1875. He probably resumed contact with the bohemian young poets of the *Cercle Zutique* (*Zutique* can perhaps be roughly translated as meaning 'cocking a snook' at the respectable world), for it was with one of the most sympathetic of them, a young Provençal poet called Germain Nouveau, that he left for London again in February. They had no money, and lived hard, taking whatever jobs presented themselves, even of the meanest sort, for there were still so many French exiles in London that it was all but impossible to find pupils for lessons in French. In the midst of this struggle for existence, Rimbaud appears to have written the final pieces for the *Illuminations*. He also renewed his card of admission to the British Museum Library, so he must have spent some time every week studying there. It was one of the darkest periods in his life.

Germain Nouveau finally left Rimbaud in June, and went back to Paris. Soon after he left, Rimbaud seems to have

*See Appendix I

experienced some kind of spiritual or physical crisis. In any case it was severe enough for his mother – who, in spite of his earlier hatred of her, never seems to have deserted him at his most difficult moments – to put her younger daughter into a convent, and hurry over to him with her elder daughter Vitalie, who was only fifteen at the time. He cannot have been desperately ill, for he went to meet them at Charing Cross, and found pleasant enough rooms for them at 12 Argyle Square. Vitalie's journal gives a picture, not of a forlorn, sick or spiritually shattered hysteric, but of a kind and solicitous son and brother, who showed them round the sights of London, including Kensington Gardens and the British Museum, and accompanied his mother on shopping expeditions where he acted as interpreter, as she could not speak a word of English. Perhaps he was just utterly lonely and disillusioned. Germain Nouveau's role in Rimbaud's life after his return to Paris remains obscure. We know that Verlaine met him in a bar at King's Cross, and in 1889 published an extremely friendly sonnet about the encounter, which may have taken place in 1875.

Rimbaud left his mother and sister in London on 31 July, saying he had at last got a new job. He was in a state of extreme sadness. Most biographers have been in accord in thinking that he went to Scotland to take up a post in a school there, but more credible evidence now suggests that he went to Reading, to teach in a coaching establishment run by a Frenchman called Camille Leclair. Little is known about this episode, except that internal evidence suggests that he was still working on the final pieces of the *Illuminations* during his life there, and also began to study music. At the end of 1874 he left England for good, shorn of all his dreams and left only with a corrosive scepticism. He went to Charleville for Christmas, and then started out on his travels. He went first of all to Stuttgart, as a paying guest with a family called Wagner. He had always had a remarkable gift for languages, and appears to have mastered German very quickly.

Meanwhile Verlaine, with remission for good conduct, had been let out of prison in January. The first thing he did was to rest with his mother in the country, in order to get used to normal life again. Then he went to Paris, still obsessed with the idea that he could make it up with his wife, in spite of the legal separation. The Mautés refused to allow him to see either Mathilde or his son. He then thought of becoming a Trappist monk, but it soon became clear to him that he had no vocation for such a life. Inevitably, his broken thoughts turned to Rimbaud. He got hold of his address in Germany from Delahaye, and went to see him in Stuttgart, but in his new proselytizing religious mood, and with Rimbaud more disillusioned than ever with their former life, the meeting was doomed from the start. He wrote sardonically to Delahaye: 'A rosary-clad Verlaine arrived here the other day, but three hours later he had denied God, and made the ninety-six wounds of our Blessed Lord bleed again.' The story goes that they went for a walk together, and had a violent quarrel. Verlaine had been drinking, to which he was now unaccustomed, and struck Rimbaud. Rimbaud, also under the influence of drink, struck back at him and felled him. He left him unconscious by the banks of the Neckar, where he was found next morning by some peasants who loaded him into their cart and took him back to the town.

It must be said that this quarrel is more likely to be legend than fact, as neither Verlaine nor Rimbaud ever made any reference to it, nor any of their friends at the time. And Rimbaud himself, in a letter to Delahaye, said that Verlaine had been '*fort raisonable*' during his four-and-a-half days' stay. It seems nevertheless almost certain that there was a row of some sort, in which Verlaine's behaviour totally betrayed his new Christian convictions. He decided to go back to Paris. The affair was at an end, though his deep and passionate attachment to Rimbaud, never wholly eradicated from his soul in spite of the many love affairs he was to have with young men in the future, surfaced again in the nostalgic poems he was to write in after years, especially in 'Laeti et Errabundi' and 'Ces Passions', with their frank declarations of the sexual pleasures they had indulged in.

For the next few years Rimbaud seems to have wandered over Europe and further afield, though nearly always returning to Charleville for part of the winter. His mother, shaken by the death of Vitalie, and by the fact that his brother Frédéric had more or less opted for the life of a ne'er-do-well, hardened again, and her relations with her other son lost the warmth that had characterized them in London. Verlaine nicknamed him '*l'homme aux semelles de vent*', and his restlessness grew with what appears to have been his rejection of poetry. It is difficult to know what he was doing at any given moment. As far as we can tell, he went from Germany to Italy, and after having crossed the Alps on foot took refuge for a while with a sympathetic widow in Milan, to whom he asked Delahaye to send a copy of the *Saison en Enfer*, as proof of his serious credentials as a writer. He left Milan for Brindisi, where he was struck down by sunstroke, and after a period in hospital was repatriated by the French Consul to Marseilles. Even more dubiously, he was said to have been enrolled there by an agent in search of volunteers for the war in Spain with the Carlists, but as soon as he had received his down-payment bolted for Paris, where according to Germain Nouveau he was seen in August; he tried to borrow money again from Verlaine but only received a pious letter in reply. After another winter at Charleville, he began to apply himself to learning Arabic, Hindustani and Russian, a clear indication of the parts of the world to which his thoughts were turning, and pursued for a time his studies in music; he made a disastrous trip to Vienna, from which he was ejected by the police as a beggar and undesirable alien; postponing his dreams of reaching the East on his own '*semelles de vent*', he enlisted in the Dutch colonial army which was about to be sent to Java, but deserted in Batavia. After that the story becomes even more obscure. The facts are not known for certain, but it seems at least probable that he came back to Europe as an ordinary seaman on a British sailing ship with a cargo of sugar; Germain Nouveau alleges that he saw him dressed as a British seaman in Paris on his way home to Charleville for the winter. His appearance had changed, which seems not in the least unlikely: he had entirely lost his boyish look, had grown a thick fair beard and his sunken cheeks looked like leather. The only thing that hadn't changed was the beautiful expression of his blue eyes. Next he tried to get to Alexandria, but his health was enfeebled and he stayed at home for a year. Then he set off for Alexandria, and made his first visit to Cyprus, which had recently been ceded by Turkey to Britain. A great deal of building work was in progress there; conditions were hard, he caught typhoid, and on his recovery he went back home. It was the autumn of 1879: he had a number of meetings with his old and most loyal (though not always uncritical) friend Delahaye, during which they discussed old days and his plans for the future. Rimbaud, who had given up his alcoholic bouts and seemed altogether a more controlled and decided character, told him there would be no more irregular and unplanned expeditions that so frequently ended in his returning home for the winter. He was going a long way away for some years, and now, at the age of twenty-five, was going to make a serious career for himself; and it would not be in literature. One can only conjecture what led to his decision: perhaps deep and final disillusionment with Verlaine; perhaps despair at not having his work appreciated in the literary circles of Paris; perhaps his ancestral peasant blood urged him at last, as he was strong, capable and intelligent, to try to make a practical success of his life. Before he left Charleville he was invited by a small group of his old friends to spend the evening with them. He told them what he had told Delahaye. He returned home early. None of them ever saw him again.

We have a considerable amount of information about Rimbaud's life after that evening, his travels, adventures, misfortunes and illnesses, chiefly from his letters home and the letters to and from his business associates in the Middle East. But it is not of prime concern to this story, as any connection with Verlaine – except for what Verlaine wrote about him in his absence – had ceased. Nevertheless one must complete the picture, even if summarily.

Rimbaud returned first of all to Cyprus, where he was put in charge of a gang of workmen who were building the new English Governor's summer residence in the mountains of Troodos. On that house there is a plaque, which reads:

ARTHUR RIMBAUD
poète et génie français

au mépris de sa renommée
contribua de ses propres mains
à la construction
de cette maison
MDCCCCXXXI

The only mistake in this tribute is that the date should be 1880. As was his wont, however, he quarrelled with his employer, and left at the end of June, travelling down the Red Sea. He was found in Aden, ill again with fever, by a French exporter of coffee, hides and guns, called Pierre Bardey. He made a favourable impression on Bardey, who gave him employment, though scarcely more than to supply his minimum needs. Bardey's ambition was to open a branch of his business in Harar, then a remote and primitive town on the other side of the Red Sea. Rimbaud's association with Harar, which he found the dreariest of places, was to last for some time, on and off, though he went back to Aden from time to time, on one occasion bringing back with him a young Abyssinian woman, with whom he lived for some months.

Meanwhile war had been in progress in Abyssinia between the Egyptians, the Dervishes, the Emperor of Ethiopia and Meneluk, King of Shoa, with the European powers playing a confused and often ill-judged game of power-politics against one another. Arms were desperately in demand, and Rimbaud decided to sink his savings in organizing a caravan of arms for Meneluk. His set-backs and sufferings were appalling, and when he finally reached his destination after months of delay and official obstruction (he was only able to set out in October 1886), he was despicably cheated by the King, who impounded his cargo and demanded the payment of debts he alleged his French predecessor had left on his death. When he finally got back to Aden, Rimbaud probably had little more left than the capital he set out with.

He made a further effort in 1888, with a new partner, to organize gun-running and other trade into the Kingdom of Shoa, and returned to Harar, which he had almost begun to be fond of after the nightmarish rigours of Aden. It is during this period that he appears to have been associated in some capacity with the highly lucrative slave-trade. Whatever the truth of this, the selling of arms and ammunition seems to have been his chief (though by no means only) occupation in the mud city that had grown under Meneluk to be the chief trading centre of the Empire. Nevertheless there is no doubt that Rimbaud was always missing opportunities and getting the worst of bargains, in spite of his sober habits, his integrity and endless capacity for work. He made no fortune, but established a reputation, that lasted for many years after his death, for generosity and lavish though unobtrusive kindness. People came to his house as if to a club to be entertained by his wit, the anecdotes of his experiences related with a cutting edge, and his lack of prejudice, racial or otherwise. He had one particular favourite, a young Harari boy, servant and constant companion, called Djami. So warm was his affection for him that he constantly spoke of him in his letters, and tried to arrange for money to be sent to him.

Then two things happened, and almost simultaneously. One was that the literary world of France suddenly discovered that he was not dead, nor had mysteriously vanished without trace, but that he was alive and in what part of the world he was to be found. Ever since his long absence and silence had started, his reputation, particularly among the young, had steadily grown. The excitement was intense. 'This time we have got hold of him!' exclaimed *La France Moderne* in February 1891. 'We know where Rimbaud is, the great Rimbaud, the only true Rimbaud, the Rimbaud of *Illuminations*.' And the editor wrote him a letter: '*Monsieur et cher poète*, I have read your beautiful poems. That explains how happy and proud I should be to see you the head of "*l'Ecole décadente et symboliste*" and a contributor to *La France Moderne*. Please be one of us.'

As far as we can tell Rimbaud did not answer this letter; but he kept it, and perhaps he would have answered it if he had been able. In any case it was useless. The final misfortune had occurred. He had fallen ill of the disease that was to kill him, whether it was cancer, or the tertiary stage of the syphilis he thought he had contracted in Harar. The misery of the last months of his life is almost too painful to relate. He had begun to hope that he might return home, and find a wife who would bear him a son. It was not to be; surely one of the most tragic ironies of his life. He began to have trouble with his right leg, with swellings above and below the knee-joint. At the same time he developed a nausea at the sight of food. The swellings spread, and soon he could hardly move his leg. He decided he must get to Aden as soon as possible. After days of horrible torture in a litter he reached the coast, and was taken to the British hospital. The doctor advised immediate amputation. Rimbaud, however, decided that he must first of all get to France and home, but when he reached Marseilles he was put into the Hospital of the Immaculate Conception. He sent a telegram at once to his family, telling them that his leg was going to be amputated and begging his mother to come as soon as possible. When the operation was over, he began, though with great difficulty and pain, to move about on crutches. 'My life is over!' he cried out. 'I'm no more than a dead tree-trunk.'

He stayed in hospital until the end of July, when he managed to get home to the farm at Roche. Then a ministering angel appeared in the person of his younger sister Isabelle, who set herself to give her crippled and desperate brother all the care and affection for which he craved, and which his mother with her dour and embittered nature was incapable of giving him. She prepared the best room in the house for him to use, and filled it with flowers. He was overcome with surprise and delight. From that moment until his death she was always at hand, all her tender nature overflowing with solicitude and love towards him. He began to take opiates, and under their influence he would tell her the story of his life and of his dreams, while he played on a harp and sang gently from time to time. He hardly ever slept for more than the briefest periods, and began to lose the use of his right arm.

He became obsessed with the idea that if he could only get back to the East the sun and the heat would bring about a gradual convalescence. A month after his return to Roche, he set off again for Marseilles, with Isabelle. Nothing, nobody could stop him. But it very soon became clear that a sea-journey was out of the question. He was taken back to the Hospital of the Immaculate Conception. There his strength, like his hope, began gradually to fade. For a short while, every evening, he seemed to rally. Isabelle began to plead with him to return to his Catholic religion. At last he yielded, and the priests came.

In his more lucid moments of the evening, he seemed to

become a *voyant* again. While awake and conscious, he described visions and hallucinations he was having. He talked of 'columns of amethyst, angels in marble and wood; countries of indescribable beauty; and he used to paint these sensations, expressions of curious and penetrating charm'. It was as if the poet of the *Illuminations* had risen again to the surface, now that all worldly ambitions had perforce left him, and his extraordinary imaginative powers were once more supreme. Isabelle had not then read the *Illuminations*, but a few weeks later she did, and was amazed to find there visions of the same order, though she claimed that what he had described to her had even greater depth and enchantment. Often, too, he talked of his caravans as if he feared to be late for their start. Sometimes he spoke of his friends and associates in Harar, and seemed to imagine that she was with him out there, sharing his adventures and his problems. Above all he talked of Djami, whose fate remains unknown.

Rimbaud died on 10 November 1891. He was only three weeks older than thirty-seven. Isabelle accompanied the coffin back to Charleville. His mother immediately instructed the parish priest to organize a funeral *de première classe* for 10 a.m. the next morning. The priest objected that there was far too little time to arrange everything properly, or to collect any of his local (let alone Paris) friends to pay their respects to his remains. She showed herself as obstinate on this matter as she had always been on so many other matters. The result was that she and Isabelle were the only mourners.

In the 1880s Verlaine was engaged in writing a number of portrait-pamphlets of contemporary literary figures (including himself) for a series called *Les Hommes d'Aujourd'hui*. One of them was of Rimbaud (published in 1888, though he later dated it 1884), with an amusing cover-drawing of Rimbaud as a small boy painting the various vowels in the colours he attributed to them in his famous poem 'Voyelles'. At that time Verlaine did not know whether Rimbaud was alive or not, only going as far as saying that he had heard rumours that he was in Aden. The portrait is warmly eulogistic, and though much of it is devoted to a summary of his career (carefully omitting Verlaine's own part in it), certain passages are of great significance, and worth quoting here. He begins by writing that:

Felix Fénéon has said, in speaking truly of the *Illuminations* of Arthur Rimbaud, that they are beyond all literature, and no doubt above it. One could apply the same judgement to the rest of his work, *Poésies* and *Une Saison en Enfer*. One could even follow that judgement up to put Rimbaud in a certain sense outside the whole of human experience, and above ordinary life altogether. So gigantic is his work, so completely did he make himself free, so proudly was his life passed, so proudly that one has no news of him, and one doesn't even know whether he is still alive. The whole story is as simple as a virgin forest and as beautiful as a tiger. . .

Many opinions have been expressed on Rimbaud as a person and as a poet. Some maintained this or that, one person went so far as to say: 'But he's the Devil !' He was not the Devil, nor bad, he was Arthur Rimbaud, that is to say a very great poet, absolutely original, of an unique flavour, prodigious master of language – a boy most certainly not like the rest of the world, but clear, straight-forward without the slightest malice, whose life, so grotesquely compared to that of a werewolf, above all existed in light and strength, beautiful in its logic and strength as his work. . .

[Verlaine goes on to quote 'Veillées' and 'Aube' from the *Illuminations*]

One should beware of the portraits one has of Rimbaud, including the drawing on this pamphlet, artistic and amusing as it is. Rimbaud, at the age of sixteen or seventeen, a time when he was writing the poetry and at work on the prose one has before one, was on the contrary beautiful – indeed very beautiful – rather than ugly, which is proved by the picture one has of him by Fantin in his 'Coin de Table'. A kind of sweetness and smiling air radiated from his eyes of a cruel pale blue colour, and hung about his strong red lips with their bitter lines: mysticism and sensuality – and to what a degree! One day perhaps one will find pictures that will give some closer idea of his true appearance. . .

After the final, almost shattering though perhaps not violent encounter with Rimbaud, Verlaine decided to go to England again, and find employment as a teacher. His first engagement was at a grammar school at Stickney in Lincolnshire, where he seems to have been comparatively happy, both liked and appreciated by those who ran the school. It was at Stickney that he discovered *Hymns Ancient and Modern*, which delighted him and many traces of which can be found in his work of the period. It also seems that he discovered Tennyson, and was deeply impressed by 'In

Memoriam', and by the poems which were filled with a melancholy inspired by the autumnal landscapes of Lincolnshire.

The next year he moved from Stickney to teach French and Latin at a Catholic school in Bournemouth. In spite of the affection which he had developed for England, he left to go back to France in October 1877. He was equipped with two excellent testimonials from the English schools where he had taught, and had no difficulty in finding a post in France at the Collège Notre-Dame at Rethel, in the heart of the Ardennes, not far from Charleville and filled with memories of Rimbaud. There he wrote some of his finest poems, and fell in love with one of his pupils, Lucien Létinois, who at the age of nineteen had just completed his studies. It seems that Verlaine saw something of Rimbaud in his physical presence – though no one else did. He took him over to England, and succeeded in finding him a post at his old school of Stickney, while he himself joined the staff of a school at Lymington, just opposite the Isle of Wight. His passion for Lucien increased during their separation, and it seems likely, though far from certain, that during the Christmas break of 1879 they became, though briefly, lovers. Lucien also became, in a sense, a surrogate for Verlaine's own son Georges, whom the Mautés refused to allow him to see. After Lucien had finished his year of military service in 1883, he died of typhoid fever; an appalling end to the friendship Verlaine had hoped, one cannot help thinking, would take the place of the ruined relationship with Rimbaud. In the following years Verlaine was to write a number of pious poems in memory of Lucien, a series of twenty-five of which appeared in *Amour*.

The death of Lucien drove Verlaine to despair and, once

more, to drink. It also seems likely that he indulged in a large number of brief, promiscuous affairs, both with women and young men. At the same time he began to emerge from the clouds that had overshadowed his reputation since the Rimbaud scandals. His appreciations of Rimbaud, Corbière and Mallarmé (always a sympathetic and generous friend), which were to appear in *Les Poètes Maudits*, started to be published in the magazine *Lutèce*. They were soon followed by a number of his own poems. The younger generation sat up and took notice, and a cult for Verlaine, and the poets he wrote about with such enthusiasm, began, out of which the so-called 'Decadent' movement found its inspiration, and later the *Symbolistes*. Late in December 1884 *Jadis et Naguère* was published, and though it contained few completely new poems, it proved to be just what the younger poets were looking for.

Verlaine's next (and apparently final) male infatuation was for a young artist Frédéric-Auguste Cazals, who was about twenty or twenty-one when they met. They were drawn to one another from their first meeting, on an impulse of Cazals', but the boy was not homosexual and rebuffed Verlaine when he made sexual advances to him. Nevertheless he was light-hearted and amusing, and endlessly ready to help and work for the ailing and perennially penniless poet in whatever way he could. He was exactly the kind of admirer Verlaine was in need of, and though it was painful to him to have to sublimate the sexual desire Cazals aroused in him, they remained very close to one another to the end; though there seems to have been a period of at least partial estrangement between the summer of 1890 and January 1891. He wrote a poem to him which appeared in *Bonheur*, and begins:

Mon ami, ma plus belle amitié, ma meillure,
'Les morts sont morts, douce leur soit l'éternité.'
Laisses-moi te le dire en toute vérité,
Tu vins au temps marqué, tu parus à ton heure . . .

It was at this period of his life when Cazals entered it, that
Verlaine began to suffer from serious ulcers and had to have
them treated in hospital; they were possibly from a late stage
of syphilis, but other maladies attacked him at the same
time. During the nine years from 1886, when he was only
forty-one, if one adds all the periods of hospital treatment
together, he spent about four years in hospital; brave, if
sometimes deeply dejected, writing a great deal and often
visited by the ever larger number of his admirers, many of
whom supported him financially. They included a new rich
devotee, Robert de Montesquieu, who is supposed to have
been the original of Charlus in Proust's *A La Recherche du
Temps Perdu*. The hospital he most frequently returned to,
in fact became almost a pensioner of, was the Broussais.
Another new admirer was Huysmans, whose *A Rebours*
contributed not a little to making Verlaine known to a wider
public.

Verlaine's mother, who had always remained so devoted
to her errant son, died in January 1886, leaving very little of
the family money. The poet, who had always needed a
maternal bosom to lean on, and with the homosexual side
of his nature frustrated by Cazals, took up with two
mistresses, both prostitutes or near prostitutes: Philomène
Boudin, whom he called Esther, and Eugénie Krantz. They
both exploited him ruthlessly, whenever there was anything
to exploit, but Eugénie was the kinder and more considerate
of the two.

His fame was growing all the time. His new publisher, Léon Vanier, published *Parallèlement* in 1889, which showed a very different spirit from *La Bonne Chanson* and *Sagesse*, frankly acknowledging homosexuality and denouncing Mathilde for her cruelty and hypocrisy. It contained the famous poem about Rimbaud which I have already quoted, with the poignant lines:

> Je n'y veux rien croire. Mort, vous,
> Toi, dieu parmi les demi-dieux!
> Ceux qui le disent sont des fous,
> Mort, mon grand péché radieux. . .

At the time he wrote the poem he still clung to the idea that Rimbaud might still be alive; though even if he were dead, he was forever alive in his heart. Verlaine took a cure at Aix-les-Bains, then went back to Broussais. In 1890 a new book of poems, *Dédicaces*, was published, which showed little of Verlaine's true inspiration, rather a slow, sad decline in his powers.

In his last years, beginning in 1892, Verlaine undertook a series of lecture tours in Holland, Belgium and England. The lectures consisted mainly of recitations of his poems, interspersed at random with reminiscences and anecdotes; the literary world came to see the famous poet as well as to hear him, and in most places these 'lectures' formed a great attraction. In Holland he lectured in The Hague, Leyden and Amsterdam: a tour that lasted nearly a fortnight, and brought him some much-needed money. His success in Holland encouraged him to suggest to a circle of avant-garde artists in Belgium that he should do a similar tour in that country. The suggestion was taken up with enthusiasm, and he arrived in Charleroi on 25 February, after another spell in hospital. There he lectured to a large audience in the Eden Theatre. The following day in Brussels was, however, a disaster. His admirers had organized a dinner for him beforehand. Inevitably it went on too long, and when Verlaine arrived at the lecture-hall he was not only extremely late, but drunk: he tripped as he climbed to the platform, and his papers were scattered all over the room. The result was a muddled and largely incoherent address, which did not go down at all well with the restive audience. This was followed by far happier occasions in Antwerp, Liège and Ghent. The most remarkable of his appearances was before the Junior Bar of Brussels, in the same *Palais de Justice* where he had suffered his humiliations twenty years before. Daringly – and not uncharacteristically – he called his lecture *Mes Prisons*. He was in the best of form, witty and full of jokes about his earlier experiences; his gaiety and charm and frankness turned the occasion into a great triumph, so successful indeed that on his return to Paris he received a telegram from the Junior Bar congratulating him and wishing him the best of health. Alas, his health was very poor, but the doctors at Broussais got him well enough to lecture in Lorraine. Then came an invitation which pleased him more than any other: to visit and give readings in England, the country for which he had conceived such a deep affection and admiration.

The tour, which was to include appearances in Oxford and Manchester as well as London, was organized by Will Rothenstein, with the assistance of Arthur Symons, Robert Sherard and York Powell of Christ Church in Oxford. They met him at stations, assembled his admirers, put him on trains on his departures, and gave him his fees at the last moment to prevent him drinking the money away at once. As soon as he had arrived in London, and rested, he was visited, among others, by Edmund Gosse, William Heinemann, Herbert Horne and John Lane; Ernest Dowson went to hear him lecture at Barnard's Inn, and Lane pronounced the lecture a great success.

When Verlaine reached Oxford and was shown round, he fell in love with the city at once. His audience at the lecture was small but enthusiastic. In his euphoria, he wrote a poem beginning: 'O toi, cité charmante et mémorable, Oxford !'. Indeed, he was so enchanted with Oxford that it was difficult to get him on the train for Manchester. He made 1,000 francs for his London and Oxford lectures, and another 875 francs for Manchester. When he got back to London, he was fêted all round, gave a long interview for the *Sketch*, and was invited to contribute to various other periodicals. When he returned to Paris, he thought of his English tour in an unqualified glow of pleasure.

During the last phase of his life, when he was not lecturing or spending long periods in hospital, Verlaine became the habitué of a number of Left Bank cafés, in one of which he could generally be found late in the evening by his young devotees and hangers-on, who steadily increased in numbers and no doubt encouraged him to drink too much. He was now revered; sometimes the guests got up when he entered, and the police had instructions to keep away from him, except when he was in need of help. Some of those who preferred the Right Bank cafés of Montmartre used to cross to the Left Bank purely in order to see Verlaine. As one of them (Henri Duvernois) recalled at a later date, they would find him:

. . . with his old dosshouse overcoat, his vagabond's

cudgel, and his hirsute face ennobled by suffering and sadness. When some young bourgeois timidly approached him and assured him of his passionate admiration, he would retort 'In that case, Monsieur, you might oblige me with a five-franc piece!' He didn't ask for more because, with a sort of wisdom, he had reduced his needs to the level of his resources.

Another devotee, Yvanhoe Rambosson, recalled meeting him on a number of evenings in the François Ier café on the 'Boul' Miche', where:

. . . between his periods in hospital, Paul Verlaine found himself at home. Sitting in front of 'the humble ephemeral absinthe', a scarf the colour of dregs worn anyhow over a shirt that was probably flannel, a short pipe held in a gloriously threatening or insistent fist, a jeer in his damp, limp moustache, good humour in his faun's eyes, he used to talk, sometimes with gentleness, sometimes with trembling and rebellion, in a voice that was slightly husky and toneless. . .

Sometimes Leconte de Lisle, on his way to the Senate, crossed his path. They despised one another: Leconte de Lisle turned his bemonocled gaze away from the ragged bohemian with marked contempt, while Verlaine laughed and blew extra-vigorous puffs of smoke at him from his cheap cigar. But Verlaine had a curious revenge on him. In July 1894, Leconte de Lisle died at the age of seventy-six, when Verlaine (though he looked far older) was only fifty. Leconte de Lisle had not only been a member of the Académie Française, but had also held the honorific title of

'*Prince des Poètes*'. Verlaine was the favourite choice to follow him. An election was held at the Café Procope, and Verlaine, out of the votes of two hundred men of letters (most of them twenty-five years old, or younger), received seventy-seven, Herédia thirty-eight, Mallarmé thirty-six and Coppée twelve. It was a resounding victory. He gazed out of his window at the Jardin du Luxembourg, and observed: 'I have no palace, but there is my royal park.' It pleased Verlaine particularly as the best kind of consolation for the failure of his perhaps ill-advised attempt to be elected to the Académie, that society of *bien pensants*, in 1894. He received no votes at all; nor did another eminent candidate, who always kept up friendly relations with him, Emile Zola.

He had written: 'Why shouldn't I join the Assembly of the Forty? Haven't I got as good a right to the chair as anyone? I've published twelve volumes of poetry, five prose works, a play, and hundreds of articles in different papers. It seems to me that many Immortals can't boast of such a body of work.' But it is doubtful whether he seriously expected to be elected. He excused himself from the customary round of visits to those who were already among the 'Immortals' owing to his illness; and when – so the story goes – the medical staff at his hospital subscribed to buy him a top hat and the regulation dress, he had his photograph taken in all his finery, and then went and sold the lot the next day.

One doubts whether he was unduly depressed by the failure of his candidature. He knew that he had the fervent admiration of the younger generation, and his international reputation was steadily growing; and after all was he not the '*Prince des Poètes*'? But his health, after his visit to England, did not improve. The trouble with his leg seemed incurable, and in addition he had erysipelas and symptoms of diabetes.

His financial situation continued to be utterly precarious, but a group of fifteen friends agreed to subscribe ten francs each a month through *Le Figaro*, and the Ministry of Public Instruction made him a grant of 500 francs. This was followed by a further grant of the same amount during the following year; he received three grants in all.

After another break of several months which followed an obscure row, Cazals returned to him, and saw him frequently until the day of his death. But the old passionate feeling for young men was gone. After Lucien Létinois' death all that remained was the series of poems, so full of love 'for his son' as he had come to think of Lucien, of harrowingly sad memories, and a pious Christian resignation which does not always ring quite true. His emotional life was now divided between his two rapacious and quarrelling mistresses, but though he accepted at last the fact that Rimbaud was dead, one cannot help thinking that he remained supreme in his thoughts to the end. When Verlaine, after many difficulties in assembling the texts, managed to get Rimbaud's *Poésies Complètes* published in 1896, he wrote his long meditated introduction, and in October yet another article on him in *La Plume*, recalling their first meeting twenty-four years earlier.

Verlaine had not seen his son Georges since he was seven years old. He longed to see him again, but Mathilde, who had married again after the divorce had been made absolute, continued rancorously to put obstacles in the way, and the one opportunity that had a chance of success failed because of a muddle about addresses.

He was living now, with Eugénie in attendance, at 39 rue Descartes. He was aware, it seems, that he was dying. Though Eugénie claims that he had completely given up absinthe or any other strong drink, the combination of his ills sapped his remaining strength all too rapidly. On 8 January 1896, at seven o'clock in the evening, he died, a tired old man though only in his fifty-second year.

A number of his friends came round to see him on his death-bed and to pay homage, including Maurice Barrès, Mendès, de Montesquieu and Mallarmé, and his devoted younger admirer St Georges de Boutelier.

He was buried on Friday the 10th. Hundreds of poets, songwriters and other men of letters, almost all literary Paris in fact, followed the funeral procession or assembled at the church and at the cemetery afterwards.

III

An Anglo-American Episode

Robert Frost &
Edward Thomas

It was the toss of a coin, so we are told, that decided Robert Frost to go to England rather than to Vancouver. He was thirty-eight, married with four children, and though to be reckoned a poet was his deepest ambition, he had not yet had a volume published. Most poets have published a first book, even if mainly of juvenilia, before they are thirty, or perhaps twenty-five; but Robert Frost had even to come to England before the originality of his poetic gifts was recognized, and it was in London that his first book, *A Boy's Will*, was published. And it was also in London that he first met Edward Thomas: a coming together that was to have a profound effect on both writers – though their closeness to one another turned out to be fated to last only a matter of eighteen months.

He was born in San Francisco in 1874, but the roots of his family were in New England. His father died in penury and disappointment in Lawrence, Massachusetts, in 1885, and young Frost had to live with unsympathetic grandparents until his mother found work in Salem as a teacher, and moved with her family to Amherst.

During these early years Frost appears as a rather lazy, moody boy, prey to irrational fears and suspicions, and

135

capable of violent outbursts. His father's stern, old-fashioned attitude to the young boy, whom he subjected to frequent cruel beatings, did not help. During these punishments his mother fled to her room, sobbing and praying. He seems not to have known what he really wanted to do, and tried his hand not very successfully as a farmer, or perhaps one should say more precisely as a hen-keeper. When he was thirteen, however, he began to be seriously interested in reading, and, encouraged by his mother, particularly in poetry. In 1889 he entered Lawrence High School, and began to write poetry himself. His first poem was published a year later in the *Bulletin*, and in 1890, as a senior at Lawrence, he became chief editor of the *Bulletin*. In the same year he met Elinor White, whom he married four years later.

During the next few years he graduated with honour from the high school, and entered Dartmouth College, but evidently the curriculum or the atmosphere of the college was not to his liking, because he left after one semester. In 1896 he became a special student at Harvard, where he met William James and Santayana. In 1901 his small son Elliott died, a great sorrow; also his grandfather, who left him an annuity, with which he established a poultry farm in Derry, New Hampshire. All this time he was writing poetry, but with only occasional successes in finding editors to publish the poems. It was a hard, unpropitious beginning. In 1909 he began teaching at Pinkerton Academy, and held his post there for a couple of years. By 1912 he felt he needed a change: his life had run into a rut, and he thought that new scenes, new friends, might quicken the powers he believed were in him. He was bored with farming in Derry, stale in his teaching at Pinkerton. He saved up the annuities he was receiving from his grandfather's will, and decided on a move. His wife agreed to move with him and the family abroad. Luckily the toss of the coin decided him for England. Before 1912 was out, they had sailed over and found a new home in the pretty old coaching town of Beaconsfield, on high ground about halfway between London and Oxford. Very soon, on his visits to London and Harold Monro's Poetry Bookshop, he began to make new friends in the English literary world; in particular F.S. Flint and his fellow expatriate Ezra Pound. Flint proved a tirelessly helpful and loyal ally; Pound at first promoted the new American poet with all his skill and valuable connections, but did not prove quite so certain a friend.

During this time he was sifting and selecting the poems he had written during the previous decade, and chose a name for the volume he wanted now to publish. Finding a publisher was a difficult problem; it was T.P.O'Connor, one of his new literary friends, who suggested the small firm of D.Nutt, known to be interested in poetry, and run by a lady who was the daughter-in-law of the founder. She interviewed Frost, took the poems away, and finally wrote to him accepting them for publication, though on fairly onerous terms, which involved submitting to her the option on his next four books. No sensible publisher, today at least, would make such conditions, knowing that, without tricky court procedures, you cannot indefinitely keep an author who does not want to stay with you. Frost, however, in a country that was new to him and whose customs were still strange, felt he had no choice but to sign the contract.

Thus, in 1913, *A Boy's Will* was published in London, and was well received in certain influential quarters. Flint was enthusiastic, and so was Pound. W.B.Yeats was reported to be an admirer. But the critic who was to be most important in making his reputation was Edward Thomas, who reviewed the book favourably in the *New Weekly*. Early in 1913 Ralph Hodgson introduced the two men to one another at St George's Restaurant in St Martin's Lane. Thomas and Frost appeared to find an almost immediate temperamental rapport, which was to ripen very rapidly into a close friendship and a mutual influence in the lives and careers of both, especially of Edward Thomas.

A description of Frost at this time comes from Thomas's wife, Helen. 'Robert was a thick-set man, not as tall as Edward, with a shock of grey hair. His face was tanned and weatherbeaten and his features powerful. His eyes, shaded by bushy grey eyebrows, were blue and clear. It was a striking and pleasing face, rugged and lined. I remember his loose, earth-stained trousers, his brown arms and chest, his gnarled hands, his slight American accent.'

In 1913 Thomas was thirty-five, four years younger than Frost, and had already published two dozen prose books, the first of which, *The Woodland Life*, had appeared when he was eighteen, and in 1913 four more appeared, making the total nearly thirty; Frost had published none. Thomas had in addition written innumerable review notices and articles, and one can reckon that by the time of his death four years later, he had written more than a million words in such journalism. His writing never stopped, because he could not allow it to stop. In 1899 he had married Helen Noble, and by the time Frost met him he had a family of three to keep: Bronwen and Myfanwy, the two girls, and in between, Mervyn, his son. One has the appalling impression that, even though he lived cheaply enough in the country and was reasonably abstemious in drinking and smoking, the ceaseless energy he poured into journalism and the books paid very poorly at that time and commissioned or otherwise, with their meagre advances, he only just managed to keep his head above water. That situation did not change until war had broken out and he enlisted, though he was given a grant by the Royal Literary Fund in 1913 (£150) and awarded £500 in a lump sum in lieu of a Civil List pension. He did not complain, but the strain was heavy, and in 1911 he had a temporary breakdown. His books were essentially about the English countryside, which he never tired of exploring on long solitary expeditions on foot, but sometimes he undertook biographies. For instance, by the end of 1913 he had written studies of Richard Jefferies (a great favourite of his), Maeterlinck, Walter Pater, George Borrow and Swinburne. He thought of himself as, desperately, a hack writer, but in all he wrote his critical sense was alive, shrewd and perspicacious. It was not a hack biographer who wrote of Pater's style: 'If it is a question of naturalism, even an exquisite naturalism is hard to attain, when the writing, disturbed by protuberant words, has no continuous rhythm to give it movement and coherence. What Pater has attained is an exquisite unnaturalness.' He displays the same ruthless perception when he writes of Swinburne's study of Shakespeare: 'The style suggests nothing but the sonorous lips of the rhetorician; it falls without an echo into the brain.' Only in recent years, in the light of his growing reputation as a poet, has his prose, I think I am right in saying, received the attention and appreciation it always deserved.

Edward Thomas grew up into a tall, lean, good-looking man, with blue eyes that reminded many who saw them together, of Robert Frost's own. Eleanor Farjeon, who came to know him in the last four years of his life, and fell in

love with him (and admitted as much to his wife), wrote of
him on one occasion: 'To look and listen to Edward was
enough: he had a higher degree of beauty of person, voice,
and mind than I had ever known combined in anybody, or
have known since.' And on Catherine Abercrombie he
made the same impression: 'I think Edward was the most
beautiful person I have ever seen. It was quite a shock on
first meeting him unless one had been warned.' He had, as
Catherine Abercrombie noted at the same time, a strong
tendency towards melancholy – obvious enough from his
poetry – but at times it grew so deep that he had to consider
medical treatment. Undoubtedly it added to his marital
difficulties, as one can see from Helen's own record in *As
It Was*:

There were to come dark days when his brooding
melancholy shut me out in a lonely exile, and my heart
waited too eagerly to be let into the light again. When
those days came, with no apparent reason for their
coming, bringing a deep spiritual unrest and discontent,
he would be silent for hours, and perhaps stride out of the
house, angry and bitter and cruel, and walk and walk far
into the night, and come home, worn out with deadly
fatigue. When those days came my heart trembled for
what might happen, and I, suffering his terrible spiritual
loneliness, had no thought, or seeing, or hearing, for
anything but his agony and my own despair. Then my
strong body that he loved so came to my rescue, and in
hard housework, scrubbing and washing and digging in
the garden, I would force myself to *be*, so that when the
cloud lifted he would find me to welcome him. I did these
things mechanically – cooked the food, took the children

out for walks, spoke to them, picked flowers with them, but I did not know afterwards what I had done while my spirit waited in the dark.

But this was to come, and it was only now and then that I had hints of this darkness in his soul, this fierce unrest which beyond all found peace in nature, but not in me. Alone he had to be in his agony, but when he emerged from it, exhausted by God knows what bitter contest, he loved me and needed me. . .

Thomas's review of *A Boy's Will*, written before he had met Frost, was warmly praising, but when *North of Boston* came out shortly after, what Thomas wrote was much more than that: it was in fact the recognition that a new poet had appeared with a style entirely his own, the plain simplicity of which concealed a deliberate and subtle craftsmanship. He called the poems 'eclogues' himself: they are more like short stories or short dramas, told mainly in blank verse without any rhyming, but with inner harmonies that lift them, with gentle transformation, above prose narrative. *A Boy's Will* had shown unusual gifts, but also obvious debts to other writers, past and contemporary; in *North of Boston* Frost found his own voice. To Thomas it was especially exciting because, one cannot help feeling, it responded, in style and tone, to some element deep in his own nature, an impulse that was to emerge in his own poetry, which began to be written only a few months later. What Thomas stressed particularly in his reviews of the book – and he wrote more than one – was the absence of what he had been for so long at pains to eliminate from his prose writing, the *unpoetical*, what he sensed as decorative rhetoric. In his first review, in the *Daily News* in July 1914, Thomas wrote:

This is one of the most revolutionary books of modern times, but one of the quietest and least aggressive. It speaks, and it is poetry. . . These poems are revolutionary because they lack the exaggeration of rhetoric, and even at first sight appear to lack the poetic intensity of which rhetoric is an imitation. Their language is free from the poetical words and forms that are the chief material of secondary poets. The metre avoids not only the old-fashioned pomp and sweetness, but the later fashion also of discord and fuss. In fact the medium is common speech and common decasyllables.

In a later review, in August, in the *New Weekly*, Thomas developed his theme:

The effect of each poem is one and indivisible. You can hardly pick out a single line more than a single word. There are no show words or lines. The concentration has been upon the whole, not the parts. Decoration has been forgotten, perhaps for the lack of the right kind of vanity and obsession. . . Within the space of a hundred lines or so of blank verse it would be hard to compress more rural character and relevant scenery, impossible, perhaps, to do so with less sense of compression and more lightness, unity, and breadth. The language ranges from a never vulgar colloquialism to brief moments of heightened and intense simplicity. There are moments when the plain language and lack of violence make the unaffected verses look like prose, except that sentences, if spoken aloud, are most felicitously true in rhythm to the emotion. Only at the end of the best pieces, such as 'The Death of the Hired Man', 'The Black Cottage' and 'The Wood Pile', do we realize that they are masterpieces of deep and mysterious tenderness.

These particular qualities, which so deeply impressed a man never taken in by the meretricious or what was insincerely or sentimentally phrased, are well exemplified by the comparatively short 'The Death of the Hired Man', which became one of the poems most admired and most frequently quoted of Frost's early period. It is deeply felt, beautifully restrained in its pathos and understanding of the simple people of his home country, rising without strain or affectation to its high moments:

> Part of a moon was falling down the west,
> Dragging the whole sky with it to the hills.
> Its light poured softly in her lap. She saw it
> And spread her apron to it. She put out her hand
> Among the harp-like morning-glory strings,
> Taut with the dew from garden bed to eaves,
> As if she played unheard some tenderness
> That wrought on him beside her in the night.
> 'Warren,' she said, 'he has come home to die:
> You needn't be afraid he'll leave you this time.'
> 'Home,' he mocked gently.
>   'Yes, what else but home?
> It all depends on what you mean by home.
> Of course he's nothing to us, any more
> Than was the hound that came a stranger to us
> Out of the woods, worn out upon the trail.'
> 'Home is the place where, when you have to go there,
> They have to take you in.'
>   'I should have called it

Something you somehow haven't to deserve.'

'It speaks, and it is poetry. . .' Robert Frost was always a canny and at times prickly promoter and defender of his own work, but even he cannot have failed to be gratified by such perceptive and sympathetic appreciation of his second book. At about this time he attempted to define his poetic credo by an exposition of his idea about what he called 'sentence-sounds':

A sentence is a sound in itself on which other sounds called words may be strung.

You may string words together without a sentence-sound to string them on, just as you may tie clothes together by the sleeves and stretch them without a clothes line between two trees, but – it is bad for the clothes.

The number of words you may string on one sentence-sound is not fixed but there is always a danger of over-loading.

The sentence-sounds are very definite entities . . . They are apprehended by the ear. They are gathered by the ear and brought into books. Many of them are already familiar to us in books. I think no writer invents them. The most original writer only catches them fresh from talk, where they grow spontaneously.

A man is all a writer if *all* his words are definitely strung on definite recognizable sentence-sounds. The voice of the imagination, the speaking voice must certainly know how to behave, how to posture in every sentence he offers. . .

The ear is the only true writer and the only true reader. I have known people who could read without hearing the sentence-sounds and they were the fastest readers. Eye readers we call them: they can get the meaning by glances. But they are bad readers because they miss the best part of what a good writer puts into his work.

Remember that the sentence-sound often says more than the words. It may even as in irony convey a meaning opposite to the words. . .

To judge a poem or a piece of prose you go the same way to work – apply the one test – the greatest test. You listen for the sentence-sounds. If you find some of these not bookish, caught fresh from the mouths of people, some of them striking, all of them definite and recognizable, so recognizable that with a little trouble you can place them and even name them, you know that you have found a writer.

. . .There are the very regular pre-established accent and measure of speaking intonation. I am never more pleased than when I can get these into strained relation. . .

This might seem, to an experienced poet, a rather elaborate (and slightly clumsy) exposition of the obvious, but it evidently cleared Frost's mind, and underlined for himself what he was trying to do in differentiating his verse from prose without any rhetorical over-emphasis. Sentence-sounds, he seems to be saying, can be more than the sound, the music of one or two lines, and must carry on to the end of the sentence, but that of course does not eliminate the necessity of the next sentence being in musical harmony with what precedes it. What is most notable, perhaps, is the interest he declares in counter-pointing the formal structure of the verse with 'the accent and measure of speaking intonation'; but that was no great discovery, and had been a characteristic of the finest iambic verse from Shakespeare onwards. One does not have to go very far into Shakespeare to find perfect examples of what Frost meant by sentence-sounds. For instance, the Queen's advice to Hamlet:

> Do not forever with thy veiled lids
> Seek for thy noble father in the dust:
> Thou know'st 'tis common; all that lives must die
> Passing through nature to eternity. . .

Four lines which belong together in sense and development of sound or music; and where in the second and fourth line the first of the five accents falls quite naturally on the first instead of the second syllable.

In the spring of 1914 the Frosts left Beaconsfield to live in a village called Little Iddens on the Gloucestershire–Herefordshire borders. A small colony of contemporary poets had settled in the neighbourhood, Wilfred Gibson and Lascelles Abercrombie, both of them contributors to Edward Marsh's original volume of *Georgian Poetry* (1911–12), the first among them: Gibson at a cottage called 'The Old Nailshop' in Greenway, and Abercrombie also very close, near Dymock, at a house curiously called 'The Gallows', from the fact that long before a highwayman had been hanged by the front door. These poets, with Rupert Brooke an enthusiastic aider and abetter as soon as he was sent the news in Tahiti, founded a small poetry magazine which was eventually called *New Numbers*. It was Gibson and Abercrombie who persuaded Frost to join them. Thomas paid them a last visit before they moved from Beaconsfield, and came again soon after they had settled in

Little Iddens. He liked the neighbourhood, and liked the company, and soon after made plans to move there himself for the autumn and bring his family with him. War had just broken out when Helen and the children arrived. In his poem 'The Golden Room', Gibson commemorates an evening when they were all together, with Rupert Brooke, who had only recently returned to England from his travels:

. . .We all talked and laughed –
Our neighbours from The Gallows, Catherine
and Lascelles Abercrombie; Rupert Brooke;
Elinor and Robert Frost, living awhile
At Little Iddens, who'd brought over with them
Helen and Edward Thomas. In the lamplight
We talked and laughed; but, for the most part, listened
While Robert Frost kept on and on and on,
In his slow New England fashion, for our delight,
Holding us with shrewd turns and racy quips,
And the rare twinkle of his grave blue eyes. . .
Now, a quick flash from Abercrombie; now,
A murmured dry half-heard aside from Thomas;
Now, a clear laughing word from Brooke; and then
Again Frost's rich and ripe philosophy,
That had the body and tang of good draught cider
And poured as clear a stream. . .

The idyll of Dymock and Little Iddens was not allowed to last very long. The war, which had broken out in August, began, in spite of optimistic forecasts that it would be over before Christmas, to overshadow everything else. Frost and his family decided to go back to America: an open invitation to Thomas to go with them was included, but he could not make up his mind. In the end he allowed his son Mervyn to go with them, with some only vague suggestion that he might join them all later. Instead, he went on a trip round England to write about the mood and opinions of ordinary people in relation to the war. The trip took him as far as Brecon and Newcastle-on-Tyne. The articles appeared in the *English Review* a few months later. He might even then have joined the Frosts and Mervyn – he was after all thirty-six years old – if he had not managed to sprain his ankle on New Year's Day 1915, an accident which immobilized him for several weeks. On the other hand, he might have enlisted: a possibility that was constantly in his mind while he was laid up.

Meanwhile something else had happened of the utmost significance: he began to write poetry, breaking at last through the inhibitions that had held him back in spite of Frost's repeated urgings. He had purified his prose completely of all the decorative flourishes and dead phrases that he had inherited in his earlier writing from the style of the turn of the century, moving always to the complete naturalness of speech and the simplicity that could communicate lyrical feeling with scarcely a change in the tone of voice, so that poetry seemed to be the inevitable next step. And it was not only Frost's continual perceptive persuasion that brought him to cross the borderline, but also the intense awareness that the war evoked of himself as an Englishman, of belonging to the English tradition and the country of England; an awareness that he was going to be able to express most skilfully, without any jingoism or platitudinous sentiment – in fact deliberately rejecting them – in his poem 'This Is No Case of Petty Right or Wrong', written about Christmas time 1915, which concludes:

Little I know or care if, being dull,
I shall miss something that historians
Can rake out of the ashes when perchance
The phoenix broods serene above their ken.
But with the best and meanest Englishmen
I am one in crying, God save England, lest
We lose what never slaves and cattle blessed.
The ages made her that made us from the dust:
She is all we know and live by, and we trust
She is good and must endure, loving her so:
And as we love ourselves we hate her foe.

It appears to have been at the beginning of December that the first poems came. During the course of the month he wrote at least ten, including one of the best and most characteristic in his whole poetic *œuvre*, 'Old Man', about 'the hoar-green feathery herb, almost a tree, Growing with rosemary and lavender'. Robert Frost later picked it out as the most Thomasian of the lot, with its description of some obscure feeling, half-intuition, half-remembrance, that the scent evokes, no precise pictures of the past such as were evoked in Proust's mind by the taste of the *madeleine*, but equally strong though imageless, with its mysterious, melancholic last line:

As for myself,
Where first I met the bitter scent is lost.
I, too, often shrivel the grey shreds,
Sniff them and think and sniff again and try
Once more to think what it is I am remembering,
Always in vain. I cannot like the scent,
Yet I would rather give up others more sweet,

With no meaning, than this bitter one.

I have mislaid the key. I sniff the spray
And think of nothing; I see and hear nothing;
Yet seem, too, to be listening, lying in wait
For what I should, yet never can, remember;
No garden appears, no path, no hoar-green bush
Of Lad's-love, or Old Man, no child beside,
Neither father nor mother, nor any playmate;
Only an avenue, dark, nameless, without end.

By the end of the year he had also written 'The Manor
Farm' and 'The Combe', with their similar recapturing of
impalpable moods, so subtly, so simply, that one might
think, if one did not know to the contrary, that the author
was long experienced in the poetic expression of an unique
individual sensibility:

The Winter's cheek flushed as if he had drained
Spring, Summer, and Autumn at a draught
And smiled quietly. But 'twas not Winter –
Rather a season of bliss unchangeable
Awakened from farm and church where it had lain
Safe under tile and thatch for ages since
This England, old already, was called Merry.

When he began to write poetry, Thomas felt – or
pretended to feel – that he was imitating Frost too closely.
Frost protested that this was far from the truth, and pointed
out to him lines and passages that had a quality that was
undeniably Thomas's own, and in so doing strengthened
Thomas's understanding of his own poetic gift. It is

certainly true that Frost's unemphatic, undecorated style, as Thomas shows in his reviews of *North of Boston*, opened his mind to a new way of writing poetry and quickened what was only partly and uncertainly envisaged in his search for the right style for himself. One of his most successful poems, written in 1916, 'As the Team's Head Brass', is, for instance, reminiscent of Frost in its manner of combining description and conversation; but it is steeped in a different, stronger element than Frost had written at the time. And no one, in any case, but Thomas could have written 'The New House' (1915), or 'Two Houses' (1916) with its haunting, almost eerie, and perfectly judged conclusion:

> But another house stood there long before:
> And as if above graves
> Still the turf heaves
> Above its stones:
> Dark hangs the sycamore,
> Shadowing kennel and bones
> And the black dog that shakes his chain and moans.
>
> And when he barks, over the river
> Flashing fast,
> Dark echoes reply,
> And the hollow past
> Half yields the dead that never
> More than half hidden lie:
> And out they creep and back again for ever.

Reading these poems, one cannot help imagining to oneself Thomas on his long, solitary walks through the countryside, gathering these impressions in unique empathy with woods and fields, birds, wild animals and half-hidden evidence of what was long past, and transforming them all into his own music, his own not always penetrable inner life. And no one but Edward Thomas, it seems to me, could have made, in a rather different vein, the totally unexpected and daring comparison in 'Swedes':

> They have taken the gable from the roof of clay
> On the long swede pile. They have let in the sun
> To the white and gold and purple of curled fronds
> Unsunned. It is a sight more tender-gorgeous
> At the wood-corner where Winter moans and drips
> Than when, in the Valley of the Tombs of Kings,
> A boy crawls down into a Pharaoh's tomb
> And, first of Christian men, beholds the mummy,
> God and monkey, chariot and throne and vase,
> Blue pottery, alabaster and gold.
>
> But dreamless long-dead Amen-hotep lies.
> This is a dream of Winter, sweet as Spring.

The extraordinary thing is that few of his contemporaries and none of his editors seem to have been able to grasp the originality and imaginative power of the early poems which Thomas sent them. Harold Monro returned them in four days, in spite of the useful contributions Thomas had made to his *Poetry and Drama* (he also rejected 'The Love Song of J. Alfred Prufrock'). He was equally insensitive to a second selection of poems Thomas sent him in 1915.

Thomas adopted the pseudonym of Edward Eastaway (a family name), and sent his poems round to a number of other editors. All rejected them. He was dismayed, and no doubt came to the conclusion that they had nothing to say to the poetic mood of the early war years. The lack of appreciation of many of his friends was equally discouraging. W.H. Davies even thought they were by Frost (and bitterly regretted the mistake later on). The only one of his friends to show any interest, apart from Eleanor Farjeon, who had typed them out and often made useful suggestions for minor changes, was James Guthrie, who included two in his quarterly *Root and Branch* in 1915, and published a group of six at his Pear Tree Press. They were signed Edward Eastaway, and Thomas never saw any of his poems published under his own name before he was killed in 1917. A large batch (eighteen) were included in *An Annual of New Poetry* in 1917 before his death, chiefly owing to the urging of Gordon Bottomley, but they also were under the pseudonym of Eastaway, which he refused to relinquish. Nevertheless he was fundamentally undaunted, and the poems continued to pour out.

Meanwhile Frost had left for America with Mervyn in February. At a later date he said of his friendship with Thomas that he was 'the only brother I ever had. I fail to see how we can have been so much to each other, he an Englishman and I an American and our first meeting put off till we were both in middle life. We were together to the exclusion of every other person and interest all through 1914. . .'

When Robert Frost arrived back in America, he found that what was almost a miracle had occurred. When he left he had been practically unknown, but the success and the praising reviews he had received in England – particularly those from Edward Thomas – for his two books published in London, *A Boy's Will* and *North of Boston*, had gone ahead of him, and he found the literary world eager to welcome and honour him. Needless to say Frost, being Frost, was not idle to increase these first reverberations by every open and subtle means at his command. After he had settled some initial difficulties in persuading the immigration authorities to allow the young Mervyn Thomas into the States (difficulties which would of course never have occurred if his father had been with him), he paid a visit to Boston, where he was hailed as 'Boston's literary sensation of the day' and 'one of the most loveable men in the world'. He was easily persuaded to give some public readings of poems, and created for himself the image of just 'a plain New England farmer' who only wanted to be the mouthpiece of country people, whose life consisted of hard work and simple virtues.

That he was a far more complex personality and artist than these readings made him appear was an impression he was careful not to allow to surface. His habit of hogging the conversation (though more often than not with wit and charm) which Gibson had slyly (or innocently) alluded to in his poem, and the fact that both his father and mother were dead, gave his ever-present instinct for self-dramatization full rein, and as time went on he produced extravagant fantasies of his ancestry, life and struggles.

Within a few months of his return to his native country, *North of Boston* became, for a book of poetry, a best-seller. Soon after this success, and before his third book, *Mountain Interval*, appeared, he was elected a member of the National Institute of Arts and Letters. The universities, in characteristic American fashion, were not long in following this up. He accepted an invitation to join the faculty of Amherst College, and after this a similar invitation was extended to him by the University of Michigan. His fourth book, *New Hampshire*, was awarded the prestigious Pulitzer Prize. There was no doubt that he had become, in the space of a very few years, a nationally acclaimed literary figure. These triumphs, these continually accruing honours should have softened, or indeed wiped out the resentments he had felt for the years of neglect. And yet lively jealousies of his fellow poets – and therefore contestants for preeminence – continued far too long to do his reputation any good. He was jealous of Edwin Arlington Robinson, the most highly praised New England poet of his day; he was jealous of Amy Lowell, whose friendship for a time he assiduously (and falsely) cultivated, and gossiped maliciously about Sandburg, Wallace Stevens and Ezra Pound. It is not a pretty record for one who was basking in new-found and generous, if tardy, acclaim.

Perhaps to a large extent due to the wrench of parting with the Frosts, and the fact that his sprained ankle prevented him joining them, in July 1915 Thomas overcame his havering and enlisted in the Artists' Rifles. He had finished, with no enthusiasm at all, his last commissioned work, a life of the Duke of Marlborough, before he took the plunge. His early months of training appear to have left him no time to continue with his poetry, so unsympathetic and exhausting was the change to the inevitable chores of drilling, cleaning rifles and washing out lavatories, which every recruit had to undergo. However, the worst of this was over within a year, and having been awarded his second stripe he began thinking of applying for a commission. He had also begun to write poetry again. The latter part of 1915 was extremely productive, as was 1916, but when he reached France the flow stopped, and the only poem of 1917 which has survived is one written shortly *before* he embarked in January, 'The Sorrow of True Love'.

Among the new instructors in map-reading and other military arts who joined him before he was given his commission was a young artist, Paul Nash, who became a special friend. 'He is wonderful at finding birds' nests,' Thomas observed in one of his letters to Frost. Nash himself noted how often Thomas seemed to be oppressed by fits of melancholy and pessimism, but that when they were together and with other friends, 'he was always humorous, interesting and entirely loveable'. He was posted as a cadet to the Royal Artillery School in London, then to Trowbridge, where his vaccination made him feel especially low in spirits for a while. Eleanor Farjeon paid him a visit during one of his weekend leaves, and she relates that, as they were walking in the country, she asked him, 'Do you know what you are fighting for?' He picked up a lump of earth, saying, 'Literally, for this', and crumbled it between his fingers and let it fall.

Towards the end of November he was commissioned Second Lieutenant with Number 244 Siege Battery and posted to Lydd in Kent. In December he volunteered to go to the front with the next draft. The next few weeks, in between then and his departure at the end of January, he spent in saying goodbye to his friends, and had a poignant farewell with Helen. Three years later she wrote: 'The snow was deep on the ground and he soon disappeared in a thick fog, and we cooied to each other until we could not hear any more. I was left alone knowing I would never see him, never hear him, never hold him in my arms again.'

During this period he wrote several of his most beautiful and memorable poems, entirely Thomas and unlike anything anyone else could have written at that time. For instance, the poem which Helen once asserted was addressed to his mother, but seems much more likely to have been addressed to her. It begins:

> No one so much as you
> Loves this my clay,
> Or would lament as you
> Its dying day.

In this poem he was attempting something of greater difficulty than appears: a poem of ten stanzas, each stanza of four extremely short lines, with the first and third and second and fourth lines rhyming, and giving no sense of awkwardness or effort, and climaxing with a deeply moving single image, exactly right in expressing the mood of 'not loving' which is the intention of the poem. It is masterly: addressed to a particular person out of deep feeling, not at all a generalized 'love' poem, entirely without superfluous decoration, and so fulfilling the criterion of such English poetry as he had, in a long process of selection and rejection, come most profoundly to respond to. The poem continues, after its first stanza:

> You know me through and through
> Though I have not told,
> And though with what you know
> You are not bold.
>
> None ever was so fair
> As I thought you:
> Not a word can I bear
> Spoken against you.

An Anglo-American Episode

All that I ever did
For you seemed coarse
Compared with what I hid
Nor put in force.

My eyes scarce dare meet you
Lest they should prove
I but respond to you
And do not love.

We look and understand,
We cannot speak
Except in trifles and
Words the most weak.

I for the most accept
Your love, regretting
That is all: I have kept
Only a fretting

That I could not return
All that you gave
And could not ever burn
With the love you have,

Till sometimes it did seem
Better it were
Never to see you more
Than linger here

With only gratitude
Instead of love –
A pine in solitude
Cradling a dove.

An equally memorable and uniquely Thomas poem is 'Words', which expresses not only the love he had for the material of his craft, but his sense of the antiquity and yet freshness of the simplest words of the English language, particularly the words of non-Latin origin with their far deeper roots and richer associations – at any rate in his view – which he takes care to use in the poem itself:

> Out of us all
> That make rhymes,
> Will you choose
> Sometimes –
> As the winds use
> A crack in a wall
> Or a drain,
> Their joy or their pain
> To whistle through –
> Choose me,
> You English words?
>
> I know you:
> You are light as dreams,
> Tough as oak,
> Precious as gold,
> As poppies and corn,
> Or an old cloak:
> Sweet as our birds
> To the ear,
> As the burnet rose
> In the heat
> Of Midsummer:
> Strange as the races

Of dead and unborn:
Strange and sweet
Equally,
And familiar,
To the eye,
As the dearest faces
That a man knows,
And as lost homes are:
But though older far
Than oldest yew, –
As our hills are, old –
Worn new
Again and again:
Young as our streams
After rain:
And as dear
As the earth which you prove
That we love.

Make me content
With some sweetness
From Wales
Whose nightingales
Have no wings, –
From Wiltshire and Kent
And Herefordshire,
And the villages there, –
From the names, and the things
No less . . .

Perhaps one of the most beautiful poems he ever wrote, and the most completely expressive of his personality, is

'Out in the Dark', probably one of the very last he wrote before he left England for France:

> Out in the dark over the snow
> The fallow fawns invisible go
> With the fallow doe;
> And the winds blow
> Fast as the stars are slow.
>
> Stealthily the dark haunts round
> And, when a lamp goes, without sound
> At a swifter bound
> Than the swiftest hound,
> Arrives, and all else is drowned;
>
> And star and I and wind and deer
> Are in the dark together, – near,
> Yet far, – and fear
> Drums on my ear
> In that sage company drear.
>
> How weak and little is the light,
> All the universe of sight,
> Love and delight,
> Before the might,
> If you love it not, of night.

Some people have taken the line that Edward Thomas hardly wrote any poems that deal with the war, except 'As the Team's Head Brass' and 'A Private', but this is entirely to mistake the basic mood and method of his poetry. The war is there, almost always, as a dark shadow at the side of the picture, if not explicitly referred to, and runs as an undercurrent through the poetry in his intensified awareness of his attachment to his country and all it has meant to him. 'The Trumpet' has been taken as an example of the poetry of the euphoria of the early months (as Rupert Brooke's is), but in fact it was written much later, and has but a symbolical reference to the war. Thomas's own view of Brooke was expressed not only in his review of the first book, but also, distinctly more critically, in later letters to Frost, in one of which he wrote:

> I think he succeeded in being youthful and yet intelligible and interesting (not only pathologically) more than most poets since Shelley. But thought gave him (and me) indigestion. He couldn't mix his thought or the result of it with his feeling. He could only think about his feeling. Radically, I think he lacked power of expression. He was a rhetorician, dressing things up better than they needed.

In January, just before he went out to France, he was shown a copy of Frost's new book, *Mountain Interval*, and is reported to have said: 'Very good, though never better or different from *North of Boston.*'

On 9 February he reached Arras, where the build-up for a big spring offensive was taking place. It was here that he learned, in the midst of the dangerous duties in the front line which he had volunteered for, that three of his poems – under his own name – had been accepted for Harriet Monroe's *Poetry*. 'I should like to be a poet,' he wrote back to Frost, 'just as I should like to live, but I know about my chances in either case.' March was a month of almost unceasing rain, reducing the terrain they would have to cross to a quagmire, but April came in with sunny days and the hope that the worst of the mud would begin drying out. He wrote again to Frost, as it turned out the last letter he was ever to write to his American friend:

I have seen some new things since I wrote last and have had mud and worse things to endure which do not become less terrible in anticipation but are less terrible once I am in the midst of them. . . I see and hear more than I did because changed conditions compel me to go up to the very front among the infantry to do an observation and we spend nights without shells in the mud chiefly in waiting for morning and the arrival of relief. It is a twenty-four-hour job and takes more to recover from. But it is far as yet from being unendurable. . . I think I get surer of some primitive things that one has to get sure of about oneself and other people, and I think this is not due simply to being older. In short, I am glad I came out and I think less about return than I thought I should – partly no doubt I inhibit the idea of return. I only think by flashes of the things at home I used to enjoy and should again. . . I doubt if anyone here thinks less of home than I do and yet I doubt if anybody loves it more.

We expect soon to have to live in damp dug-outs for safety. We work or make others work practically all day with no rest or holidays, but often we have a quiet evening and can talk or write letters or listen to the gramophone playing 'John Peel' or worse things far. People are mostly friendly and warm, however ungenial. I am more than ten years older than four of the other five officers. They are nineteen, twenty, twenty-five, twenty-six and thirty-three years old. Those of twenty-five and twenty-six regard me as very old. I don't know if the two boys do – I get on better with them: in a sort of way we are fond of one another – I like to see them come in of a night back from some job and I believe they like to see me. What more should anyone want? I revert for ten minutes every night by reading Shakespeare's tragedies in bed with a pipe before I blow the candle out. . .

On Easter Sunday, 8 April 1917, the preliminaries of the battle of Arras had begun in earnest. Thomas was on duty with his battery in a quarry which soon came under intense shell-fire from the German lines. And yet no casualties were sustained, as if by a miracle, though one shell landed only a foot from where Thomas had taken up his position – but failed to explode. In the Mess that evening he was congratulated on his 'charmed life'. It so happened that the next morning it was Thomas's turn to man the observation post, while the final preparations for the British attack were made, the trenches packed with soldiers, at the ready with bayonets fixed. As the moment for going over the top approached, the battery commander, Frank Lushington, complained fretfully that they had had no call from Thomas at the O.P. When a call on the field telephone at last arrived, it was to tell them that Edward Thomas was dead, killed by the blast of a shell which did not wound him but literally knocked the life out of him.

After Thomas had been killed, Frost made light of his 'influence', in a straightforward and modest assessment:

Edward Thomas had about lost patience with the minor poetry it was his business to review. He was suffering from a life of subordination to his inferiors. Right at that moment he was writing as good poetry as anybody alive, but in prose form where it did not declare itself and gain him recognition. I referred him to paragraphs in his book *In Pursuit of Spring* and told him to write it in verse form in exactly the same cadence. That's all there was to it. His poetry declared itself in verse form, and in the years before he died he took his place where he belonged among the English poets.

Appendices

Main Works Consulted

Index

Appendix 1

pp. 77–8: An inadequate translation of this enigmatic poem
could be as follows:

My sad heart slobbers at the stern,
My heart that's full of filthy shag:
They aim at it with squirts of soup,
My sad heart slobbers at the stern;
Under the jeers of the whole troop
Who roar with laughter, one and all,
My sad heart slobbers at the stern,
My heart that's full of filthy shag.

The poilus with their sturdy pricks
Their coarse jokes cover it with shame!
In evening light a fresco looms
Of poilus with their sturdy pricks.
O magic waves I conjure you
Wash my heart clean so it be saved:
The poilus with their sturdy pricks
Their coarse jokes cover it with shame!. . .

pp. 108–9: A rough prose translation of these seven stanzas
could be as follows:

You know it, there is no difference
Between what you call Good and Evil,
That at the heart of each there is only suffering,
I want to break this pact that is too abnormal

There must be no more of this abominable schism!
There must be no more of paradise and hell!
Love must reign! God must die! The Devil must die!
I declare to you there must be only happiness. . .

The torch fell from his outspread hand,
And then the roar of fire broke out,
Vast quarrel of red eagles swallowed
In the black swirl of smoke and wind,

And the dying Satans were singing amid the flames,
They had understood, and they were proud and joyful
And this splendid choir of men's and women's voices
Re-echoed among the magnificent pavilions. . .

His arms outstretched towards the sky as if towards
    his brother,
A sublime smile on his lips, his excitement mounted;
When suddenly a terrible clap of thunder was heard.
The fire died out. . . Only a nightingale was singing.

The sacrifice was not accepted.
Some being strong and just assuredly
In the name of Heaven provoked, assuming the
    role of judge
In a stern sentence sent down this punishment.

Of the great palace with its hundred towers
Not a vestige remained, and out of this
    unheard-of disaster
Nothing survived, except a vanished dream.

Appendix 2

The history of the writing and publication of the texts of Arthur Rimbaud's poems, in both verse and prose, is extremely complicated and confused. I have tried here, to the best of my ability, to give a rough outline of the twists and turns in the story, though I have not attempted to judge variations in the texts, which is perhaps not yet possible, even for the most dedicated French scholar-students. No doubt Rimbaud himself would have said, '*Je m'en fiche!*' (or worse). The exact sequence of the prose poems in *Les Illuminations* will, I believe, never be satisfactorily established, though in this matter Rimbaud might have had something important to say, to elucidate the train of his thought.

The only text which presents few, if any, problems is that of *Une Saison en Enfer*, which was published by Rimbaud in his lifetime. He had, as we know, great hopes of it, but as it was received with chilly disregard in Paris, in a fit of bitter disillusionment he destroyed all copies he could lay his hands on, except those few, of course, which he had sent to his friends. One or two of these appear to have survived. Had they not, that would have been the end of this masterpiece, if, by chance, in 1901 a pile of copies had not been found in the printer's warehouse. They had lain there all those years because the bill had not been paid.

Before he broke with Izambard (over 'Le Coeur Volé'), to whom he used to send copies of his early poems, he also sent copies to a colleague of Izambard's, Paul Démeny, to whom he addressed his famous *Lettre du Voyant* (the second and longer letter) in May. In June 1871 he wrote to Démeny begging him to destroy all the poems he had sent him. Luckily, Démeny did not follow this instruction: there was at least a score of poems which Démeny held, and which might otherwise have been lost for good.

In the summer of 1872 Verlaine was in Belgium, having escaped there with Rimbaud. He wrote to his wife, Mathilde, pretending that he had met old friends of *Commune* days there, and wanted some documents which were to be found in an unlocked drawer in his room, in order to write a history of the time. Mathilde found the documents, but she also found a mass of letters, many of them from Rimbaud, which horrified her even if she did not completely understand them. Her father, Monsieur Mauté, hearing her sobbing, entered the room and seized the papers from her. He soon realized how important they would be if legal action were to be taken against Verlaine. It is probable that the manuscript of 'La Chasse Spirituelle' was among the papers he took possession of. It was never found again.

When Verlaine was let out of prison, as we know he visited Rimbaud in Stuttgart, where Rimbaud handed over to him prose poems he had been working on in London (and probably earlier as he had finished with literature in 1873). He asked him to send them to Germain Nouveau, in the hope that he might be able to find a publisher. They were evidently part of *Les Illuminations*. When Verlaine later met Nouveau in London, he failed, for one reason or another, to get repossession of the manuscripts. He wrote to claim them several times, and it would appear that Nouveau handed them back to him when they met again in August 1877.

In 1886, in the fifth to ninth issues of *Vogue*, a large mass of Rimbaud's poems, including prose poems from *Les Illuminations*, were published, but it remains obscure where they came from.

Meanwhile Charles de Sivry, Mathilde's brother and always on the whole sympathetic to Verlaine, appears to have obtained possession of the surviving Rimbaud poems still in the hands of the Mautés, and let Verlaine have them (as a loan?) in 1878. Later in the same year it would seem that Verlaine let Sivry have them back, together with what he had of *Les Illuminations*, in the hope that he could find a publisher – but return them to him if his efforts failed. Sivry tried to persuade his sister to let Verlaine have them for good, but she categorically refused to allow this. Verlaine would publish them? No, that was unthinkable.

In 1883 the name of Rimbaud began to be heard again among the younger literary enthusiasts of Paris. *Voyelles* and *Bateau Ivre* appeared in print for the first time. Verlaine's *Les Poètes Maudits*, which contained them, created a sensation in the new generation.

When Verlaine wrote his essay on Rimbaud in *Les Poètes Maudits* (1883–84) he didn't know whether he was dead or alive. In addition to 'Voyelles' and *Bateau Ivre*, he also printed 'Oraison du Soir', 'Les Assis', 'Les Effarés' and 'Les Chercheuses de Poux', together with some fragments of other poems and a few lines from the poems which appear in *Une Saison en Enfer*, the name and address of whose publisher he gives, though he doesn't appear to have had a copy at the time. He makes an appeal to anyone who may have manuscripts of 'Les Veilleurs', 'Accroupissements', 'Le Coeur Volé, 'Douaniers', 'Les Mains de Jeanne-Marie' and 'Soeurs de Charité', to let him have copies.

In his later essay, included in the pamphlet series of *Les Hommes d'Aujourd'hui*, he continues to lament his failure to obtain copies of five of the poems he had previously mentioned, though he now prints 'Le Coeur Volé', and 'Tête de Faune', a poem which he had not referred to before. He also quotes two prose pieces, 'Veillées' and 'Aube'.

During the autumn of 1885 a new visitor appeared in Verlaine's rooms, where he was being looked after by his mother. This was Georges Izambard, who presented himself as the former teacher of Rimbaud at Charleville, and produced a mass of papers relating to the youth of the poet, letters and above all poems, including 'Ophélie', 'Le Châtiment de Tartufe', 'Vénus Anadyomène', 'Ce Qui Retient Nina', 'Comédie en Trois Baisers', 'A la Musique', 'Le Forgeron' and perhaps others. Overwhelmingly excited, Verlaine sent them to his publisher Vanier, a totally imprudent gesture. Further difficulties about publication followed.

Fame is followed by forgeries and fakes. In the autumn of 1886 *Le Décadent* published several poems which were patently not his work. It was not until 1888 that a new discovery was made, of twenty-five authentic poems dating from Rimbaud's earliest years as a poet.

In 1891 a young poet by the name of Rodolphe Darzens, who had been thrilled by *Les Poètes Maudits* and subsequently spent much time researching Rimbaud's life and collecting copies of his works wherever he could, had an edition of his poems published, but without authorization and without the knowledge of the poet, who was in fact still alive though in the last stages of his illness in the hospital in Marseilles.

An edition was advertised, with an introduction by Verlaine, soon after the poet's death was formally announced by the *Echo de Paris*. Rimbaud's sister Isabelle got hold of the text, was appalled, and refused permission to publish. She alone now stood in the way as Mathilde had remarried and her brother persuaded her that as she no longer bore the name of Verlaine, the publication of her brother's works could do her no harm.

It was in 1895, four years after the poet's death, and only shortly before Verlaine's own death, that Isabelle at last allowed Verlaine to fulfil the dream he had entertained for so many years, of publishing Rimbaud's complete works under his own supervision. He wrote a new introduction, correcting mistakes and misapprehensions which appeared in what he had written before. He also wrote several articles, for English as well as American periodicals, to acclaim and boost the book. It was hardly necessary, so great was the reverence for Rimbaud in the new generation. The success was a triumph for the ageing poet over all the ill-intentioned and virulently prudish attitudes of the past, and one of the happiest events of his final years.

The most reliable edition of Rimbaud's work is that prepared by Jules Mouquet and Roland de Renéville for the Pléiade series in 1946 and reprinted with revisions several times since.

Main Works Consulted

I

Marchand, Leslie A. (ed.), *Byron's Letters and Journals* Vols VII–XI (John Murray, 1981)

Marchand, Leslie A., *Byron: A Biography* Vols II & III (John Murray, 1957)

White, Newman Ivey, *Shelley* Vols I & II (Secker & Warburg, 1947)

Buxton, John, *Byron and Shelley* (Macmillan & Co., 1968)

Cline, Professor Clarence, *Byron, Shelley and Their Pisan Circle* (John Murray, 1952)

Trelawny, E. J., *Recollections of the Last Days of Shelley and Byron* (London, 1858)

II

Rimbaud, Arthur, *Oeuvres Complètes* (Pléiade)

Rimbaud, Arthur, *A Season in Hell* (*Une Saison en Enfer*), transl. by Norman Cameron with drawings by Keith Vaughan (John Lehmann, 1949)

Starkie, Enid, *Arthur Rimbaud* (Faber & Faber, revised ed., 1961)

Verlaine, *Oeuvres Poétiques Complètes* (Pléiade)

Richardson, Joanna, *Verlaine* (Weidenfeld & Nicolson, 1971)

Petitfils, Pierre, *Verlaine* (Editions Juilliard, 1981)

Verlaine, *Les Poètes Maudits* (in *Oeuvres Poétiques Complètes*, op. cit.)

III

Thomas, George (ed.), *Edward Thomas: Collected Poems* (Faber & Faber, 1961)

Cooke, William, *Edward Thomas: A Critical Biography* (Faber & Faber, 1970)

Thomas, Helen, *As It Was – World Without End* (Faber & Faber, 1926, 1931)

Farjeon, Eleanor, *Edward Thomas, the Last Four Years* (Oxford University Press, 1958)

Letters from Edward Thomas to Gordon Bottomley

Thompson, Lawrance, *Robert Frost, the Early Years* (Holt, Rinehart and Winston, 1966)

Thompson, Lawrance, *Selected Letters of Robert Frost* (Holt, Rinehart and Winston, 1964)

Collected Poems of Robert Frost (Jonathan Cape, 1971)

Index

Index

'Le Coeur Volé' (Rimbaud), 77–8, 80, 172, 174
'Le Coin de Table' (Fantin-Latour), 87–8, 121
Coleridge, Samuel Taylor, 33
'The Combe' (Thomas), 150
Commune, 72, 78, 89, 90, 96, 172
Corbière, Tristan, 123
'Crimen Amoris' (Verlaine), 107–9
Cros, Charles, 85

Daily News, 141–2
Darzens, Rodolphe, 175
Davies, Scrope, 11
Davies, W. H., 153
Dawkins, British Consul, 43, 46, 58
'The Death of a Hired Man' (Frost), 142, 143–4
'Decadent' movement, 123, 175
Dédicaces (Verlaine), 125
Defence of Poetry (Shelley), 51
Delahaye, Ernest, 73, 76, 83, 102, 111, 112, 113–14
Démeny, Paul, 80, 172
Detached Thoughts (Byron), 32
Dionigi, Signora Marianna, 25
Don Juan (Byron), 12, 24, 28, 29–30, 31, 42
Don Juan (renamed Ariel: Shelley's boat), 49–50, 53, 55–6
'Le Dormeur du Val' (Rimbaud), 75
Dowson, Ernest, 127
Duvernois, Henri, 127–8

England:
  Rimbaud and Verlaine in, 90–5, 96–7, 109–10, 121–2, 126–7; Robert Frost in, 137–47

Farjeon, Eleanor, 139–40, 153, 156
Fénéon, Felix, 120

Fêtes Galantes (Verlaine), 71
Les Fleurs du Mal (Baudelaire), 70
Flint, F.S., 137
Florence, 26–7, 28, 43, 45
Foggi, Elena, 16, 19, 22
Foggi, Paolo, 22
La France Moderne, 117
Frost, Elinor (née White), 136, 147
Frost, Elliott, 136
Frost, Robert, 2, 135–55, 162–5
  early years and marriage, 135–6; and death of son Elliott, 136; moves to Beaconsfield in England, 137; first meeting with Thomas, 138; 'sentence-sounds' of, 144–6; moves to Little Iddens, 146–7; returns to USA on outbreak of war, 147, 153; and literary success, 153–5; Thomas's letters to, 162–4

Gamba family, 28, 54, 65
Gamba, Pietro, 42, 44, 54
Gautier, Théophile, 83
Geneva, 7–8
Georgian Poetry, 146
Ghill, André, 76
Gibson, Wilfred, 146, 147, 154
Gisborne, Maria, 14, 27, 32, 38
Godwin, Mary Wollstonecraft see Shelley, Mary
Godwin, William, 49
'The Golden Room' (Gibson), 147, 154
Gosse, Edmund, 127
Guiccioli, Contessa Teresa, 25, 27–8, 29, 31, 32, 42, 43, 44, 54, 65
Guthrie, James, 153

Hay, Captain John, 35, 44, 45
Heinemann, William, 127
Hellas (Shelley), 33–4

180

Index

Index

Index

'La Rivière de Cassis' (Rimbaud), 95

Roberts, Capt. Daniel, 40, 53, 55

Robinson, Edwin Arlington, 155

Roche, Rimbaud's home in, 96, 101, 107, 118

Romances sans Paroles (Verlaine), 92

Rome, 19–20, 24, 25–6, 58

Root and Branch (quarterly), 153

Rothenstein, William, 126

Rousseau, Jean-Jacques, 7, 8, 50, 51

Sagesse (Verlaine), 125

St Georges de Boutelier, 131

Une Saison en Enfer (Rimbaud), 92, 95, 101, 102–7, 112, 120, 171–2, 174

Santayana, 136

San Terenzo, 48–9, 54

Sardanapalus (Byron), 28

Shelley, Clara, 19, 22

Shelley, Elena Adelaide, 22

Shelley, Harriet (*née* Westbrook: first wife), 6, 13

Shelley, Mary (*née* Wollstonecraft Godwin: second wife), 6, 10, 13, 32, 50; in Switzerland, 7–8, 10–11; and Italian tour, 15–16, 18, 19, 22, 25–7; death of daughter Clara, 19, 22; death of son William, 26; in Pisa, 27, 28–9, 31, 35, 36, 38, 41, 42, 43, 44, 48–9, 50; miscarriage (1822), 51–2; and death of Shelley, 58

Shelley, Percy Bysshe, 2, 5–66; in Switzerland, 7–11, 12; negotiates publication of *Childe Harold* for Byron, 11–12; Italian tour, 15–27; and visits Byron in Venice, 16–19; death of daughter Clara, 19; birth of

Elena Adelaide, 22; moves to Pisa, 27; and Pisan Circle, 27, 28–54; his friendship with Jane Williams, 41–2; Masi incident, 43–7; death of Allegra, 47; hallucinations of, 47–8, 52; new boat (*Don Juan*), 49–50; Mary has miscarriage, 51–2; arrival of Leigh Hunt, 52–4; death, and cremation of, 54–66

Shelley, Percy Florence, 26

Shelley, Sir Timothy, 26

Shelley, William, 20, 26

Sherard, Robert, 126

Sivry, Charles de, 93, 173

Smith, Horace, 13–14, 33, 50

'The Sorrow of True Love' (Thomas), 156

Southey, Robert, 31

Staël, Mme de, 11

'Stanzas Written in Dejection near Naples' (Shelley), 23, 24

Starkie, Enid, 88

Stevens, Wallace, 155

Stickney grammar school, Verlaine teaches at, 121–2

'Swedes' (Thomas), 152

Swinburne, Algernon, 139

Symbolism, 71, 93, 123

Symons, Arthur, 126

Taaffe, John, 34–5, 43–4, 45–7

Tennyson, Alfred Lord, 121–2

'This Is No Case of Petty Right or Wrong' (Thomas), 148–9

Thomas, Bronwen, 138

Thomas, Edward, 2, 135, 138–65; reviews of Frost's work, 138, 141–3, 151, 153; and first meeting with Frost, 138; prose writings, 138, 139; melancholy nature of, 140–1; outbreak of war (1914), 147–8; begins to

Index

write poetry, 148–52; and editors reject his poems, 152–3; and pseudonym of Eastaway, 152, 153; enlists in Army, 155–6; sent to Western Front, 162–4; and killed at Arras (1917), 164

Thomas, Helen, 138, 140–1, 147, 156, 157

Thomas, Mervyn, 138, 148, 153, 154

Thomas, Myfanwy, 138

Tighe, George William, 27

'To Edward Williams' (Shelley), 42

'To Jane' (Shelley), 41

Todd, Dr John, 45

Tre Palazzi di Chiesa, Pisa, 31, 36

Trelawny, Edward John, 20, 36–7, 38, 40, 42, 43, 44, 50, 65; *Recollections* of Shelley's death, 55–64

'The Triumph of Life' (Shelley), 50–1

'The Trumpet' (Thomas), 162

The Two Foscari (Byron), 28

'Two Houses' (Thomas), 151

Vacca, Dr, 27, 43

Valperga (Mary Shelley), 38

Vanier, Léon, 125, 174

Venice, 13, 16–19, 21, 24

Verlaine, Captain, 69

Verlaine, Mme Elisa, 69, 96, 99–100, 124

Verlaine, Georges, 88, 122, 130

Verlaine, Mme Mathilde (*née* Mauté), 72, 85, 86, 88–90, 97, 99, 100, 111, 130, 172, 173, 175

Verlaine, Paul, 2, 69–73, 76, 85–131, 172–6; early years and poetry, 69–71; marriage to Mathilde, 72; invites Rimbaud to Paris, 73, 83, 85–6; birth of son Georges, 88; leaves his wife and home, 89–90; in England, 90–5, 96–7, 109–10, 121–2, 126–7; leaves Rimbaud, 97–100; shoots Rimbaud and sent to prison, 100–1; released from prison, 111; visits Rimbaud in Stuttgart, 111–12, 172–3; portrait-pamphlet of Rimbaud, 119–21; infatuation for Lucien Létinois, 122; and for Cazals, 123–4; illness of, 124, 127, 129; death of mother, 124; lecture tours, 125–7; frequents Left Bank cafés, 127–8; elected '*Prince des Poètes*', 128–9; death of, 130–1

Villa Diodati, Coligny, 8, 13

Villa Dupuy, Montenegro, 48, 53–4

Villa I Cappucini, Este, 16, 18–19

Villa Pliniana, Lake Como, 16

Viotti, Lucien, 72

The Vision of Judgement (Byron), 31

Vivian, Charles, 55

Viviani, Emilia, 42

La Vogue, 93, 173

'Voyelles' (Rimbaud), 83, 120, 173, 174

Williams, Edward E., 27, 35, 36, 38–53 *passim*; death and cremation of, 54–65

Williams, Jane, 27, 35, 36, 37, 38, 41–2, 43, 49, 52, 54

Wollstonecraft, Mary, 27, 32

The Woodland Life (Thomas), 138

'Words' (Thomas), 159–60

Wordsworth, William, 9–10

Yeats, W.B., 137–8

Zola, Emile, 129

184

3 LITERARY FRIENDSHIPS

Again, as in *The Strange Destiny of Rupert Brooke*, John Lehmann shows himself a master of biographical narrative and literary appreciation. His theme is the way in which two outstanding and gifted poets will come together and for a number of years influence one another in their lives and their art. He has chosen three exemplary, if very different friendships. First, the coming together of Byron and Shelley in Switzerland and Italy, at a time when both were approaching the height of their powers. Second, in the 1870s in France, the fatal conjunction of Verlaine, husband and father, and the precocious young genius Rimbaud, who fled away together in circumstances as scandalous as they were poetically productive. Third, the friendship in England between Robert Frost, thirty-eight and still unrecognized in his own country, and the English writer Edward Thomas, who had only written prose until then, but who, soon after this friendship began, started to write the poems that have